My friend Chuck Colson worked tird-
view on the sacredness of life, the sa ious
liberties. But he had much more to s t are
now clamoring for the center stage i d
eloquently and powerfully in *My Final Word*!

—Joni Eareckson Tada,
Joni and Friends International Disability Center

After accepting Jesus Christ as Lord and Savior, Chuck Colson blessed
the Christian community, our nation, and the world with an enormous
fund of timeless wisdom. I'm delighted that many of his essays and
memos have been gathered together in *My Final Word*. These reflections
by one of the great Christian witnesses of our time will be read with
profit for many decades to come.

—Robert P. George, McCormick Professor of Jurisprudence,
Princeton University

Every man's "final words" are important, but Chuck Colson was no
ordinary man. Chuck's "words" slice through the fog and clutter of this
culture and authoritatively speak to a dozen of the most compelling
issues of our day. This is a must-read for anyone who wants to survive
the current cultural tsunami.

—Dr. Dennis Rainey, host of *FamilyLife Today*

A great encore. Chuck's fervent joy in being freed by Christ shines
through all his slashing critiques of contemporary trends.

—Marvin Olasky, editor-in-chief, *World*

Chuck Colson was a prison-reformer-turned-cultural-transformer. When
he left this world for a better one in 2012, he left behind a legacy of sacrificial love and many words of wisdom we still need to hear. This book is
filled with such words. They still stir, inspire, and give us hope.

—Timothy George, founding dean of Beeson Divinity School
of Samford University, and general editor of the Reformation
Commentary on Scripture

Chuck Colson's voice is still heard on the issues of today. In *My Final Word* he has addressed every issue that confronts the world today. In addition to his wealth of knowledge, experience, and love for Christ, his archival material reveals prophetic insight into how believers in America are going to face persecution because of their faith. Dr. Colson sounds the alarm for the church to ready itself for battle—a necessary part of standing for Jesus Christ and the Word of God in the last days. You will be challenged in your Christian faith, but you will also be blessed by understanding how the gospel is moving forward in troubled times, to bring others to salvation for the glory of our Lord and Savior.

—Franklin Graham, president and CEO,
Billy Graham Evangelistic Association; Samaritan's Purse

# MY
# FINAL
# WORD

# Also by Charles Colson

*The Faith* (with Harold Fickett)
*Loving God*
*God and Government*
*Doing the Right Thing* DVD

# MY
# FINAL
# WORD

## HOLDING TIGHT
## TO THE ISSUES THAT MATTER
## MOST

EXPANDED EDITION

## CHARLES W. COLSON
WITH ANNE MORSE

Foreword by Eric Metaxas

ZONDERVAN

*My Final Word*
Copyright © 2015, 2017 by the Chuck Colson Center for Christian Worldview

This title is also available as a Zondervan ebook.

Requests for information should be addressed to:
Zondervan, 3900 *Sparks Dr. SE, Grand Rapids, Michigan 49546*

This edition: ISBN 978-0-310-53450-1

The Library of Congress has cataloged the hardcover edition as:

Colson, Charles W.
     My final word / Charles Colson with Anne Morse.
          p. cm.
     Includes bibliographical references and index.
     ISBN 978-0-310-52064-1 (hardcover, jacketed)
     1. Christian sociology—United States. 2. Christianity and politics. 3. United
States—Moral conditions. I. Morse, Anne. II. Title.
BT738.C642 2015
230—dc23                                                                    2015001064

*Cover design: Tammy Johnson*
*Cover photography: Prison Fellowship*
*Interior design: Dan Dingman*

*Printed in the United States of America*

16 17 18 19 20 /DHV/ 20 19 18 17 16 15 14 13 12 11 10 9 8 7 6 5 4 3 2 1

# CONTENTS

# FOREWORD

Anyone who had the privilege of knowing Chuck Colson personally misses him greatly, and I'm humbled to be included in that blessed group. But truth be told, people who only met Chuck once—whether in a prison or in a book-signing line or elsewhere—miss him as well, and I assume that if you are reading this book now—and have read his other books over the years—you miss him too. But this book is good news for all of us who miss Chuck Colson. That's because the pieces included herein are about as personal as anything Chuck ever published. They're taken from the very memos he wrote on an illimitable array of subjects, and they give the reader the sense that the man who thought these thoughts and wrote them and spoke them is at your elbow, passionately and urgently and compellingly expressing them to you as you read them.

What this book contains is vintage Colson. There is so much here on such a breadth of vital topics that I pray Americans would read this book and reread it and study it in small groups until they know it and are as passionate about these things as Chuck was himself. In fact, I would dare say that if enough Americans familiarized themselves with what's in this book, the American church would dramatically change for the better, which would mean that America would dramatically change for the better. That's not some vain hope; there is gold in these pages. Avail yourself of it.

Just a few weeks ago I had the privilege of lunch with Chuck's widow, Patty Colson, in the home she and Chuck shared in Naples, Florida. As you walk into their living room through the entrance hall you can be excused for gawking at the memorabilia on the wall. There's an original pen-and-ink drawing of one of the most famous political cartoons of the Watergate era, of Chuck decked out in a monk's habit holding a "The End Is Nigh" sign and a hunched Nixon walking past with a shocked look of recognition on his face. A bit farther on there are photos of Chuck with popes and presidents—and with just about everyone else you can think of this side of King Canute and Julius Caesar.

But then you come to the bookshelf. It is very tall, and it's packed with volumes you can tell he read and treasured. Those books tell you far more about Chuck than the memorabilia and photos. Chuck was very well read and voraciously inquisitive. I was cheered to see books by Aleksandr Solzhenitsyn and Fyodor Dostoevsky and Paul Johnson and William F. Buckley and Whitaker Chambers and C. S. Lewis, and of course there were books by Richard Nixon and books by Chuck himself too. There were also biographies of Jonathan Edwards and Edmund Burke and John Adams and Winston Churchill. Seeing my biography of Bonhoeffer there among those other books seriously flummoxed me— which is to say, it thrilled and embarrassed me both.

After a wonderful lunch with Patty and our mutual friend Martha Linder, my visit was giddily punctuated when Patty generously gave that book to me to take home. I can hardly bear the terrible honor of that. It is the very same dog-eared and copiously annotated copy that Chuck proudly showed me when I visited him there four years before. I could hardly then believe that this man whom I so revered had so thoroughly engaged with my telling of Bonhoeffer's life. To be able to look at what he wrote in response to what I wrote will be like having a conversation with him all over again, one that can go on forever. But Chuck's notes and scribblings in its pages and in the pages of all the books on that bookshelf say most of what needs saying about this great man: that ideas were everything to him and that he engaged deeply with whatever he read. In fact, he almost seems to have wrestled every book the way Jacob wrestled the angel on the plain of Penuel, refusing to let go until the angel blessed him. The thoughts in the book you hold in your hands now are a testament to that.

My solemn charge to you then, dear reader, is that you would read this book as Chuck read the books on his bookshelf. Wrestle with this as you read it, and don't let it go until it blesses you, as it is meant to do and surely will. Let it mark you forever, as the angel marked Jacob, and may others see how it has changed you by the way you walk through life hereafter.

Eric Metaxas, November 2014

# INTRODUCTION

"Anne! It's Chuck! How ya doin'?"

That staccato voice was familiar from the nearly eighteen years I'd worked at Prison Fellowship Ministries as a writer for the radio program *BreakPoint*. Chuck Colson, the one-time Watergate felon who'd founded Prison Fellowship Ministries after getting out of prison himself, was my boss. I grabbed a pen and pad of paper to scribble notes on his latest idea for the daily, four-minute *BreakPoint*.

Since Chuck's death on April 21, 2012, many have written about his days as a White House "hatchet man," his dramatic conversion to Christianity, and his founding of an international ministry. But few people know what it was like to work with him on writing projects.

Chuck began *BreakPoint* in order to help Christians think "Christianly" about everything from embryo-destructive research and animal rights to art, marriage, music, and Darwinism. He enjoyed few things more than his monthly meetings with his team of writers, who worked with him on *BreakPoint* radio scripts and on his *Jubilee* and *Christianity Today* columns. He always came into the second-floor conference room smiling, asking, in his booming voice, how we were, moving around the big table to shake hands with us and ask how our kids were doing.

After a prayer, Chuck was eager to hear our ideas for what he could talk about on the radio and write about in his columns. He enjoyed the sometimes boisterous intellectual debates—he never wanted anyone to be a "yes man" or "yes woman"—and he relished attacking any flaws in our reasoning, whether the subject was the latest film, a new book, something the current US president had said, or what various special interest groups were up to.

Animal rights lobbyists in particular drove Chuck crazy. He always wanted to comment on the latest uproar—such as the time the People for the Ethical Treatment of Animals claimed Jesus was a vegetarian. Chuck's writers would often e-mail around the latest story in which one celebrity or other announced that animals had the same value as people (if not more), and that a law ought to be passed to that effect, but we did our best to keep them away from Chuck, lest we find ourselves drafting yet another script on the subject.

Chuck frequently came to our meetings with fresh stories from his travels around the world—a chance encounter, perhaps, at an airport with someone who had read one of his books and recognized the figure in the neat suit and big, black-framed glasses. He couldn't wait to tell us about a conversation he'd had with a prison inmate in a developing country or an atheistic political leader he'd encountered in Eastern Europe and with whom he'd shared the gospel.

If Chuck came up with a *BreakPoint* idea between monthly meetings (often sparked by something he'd read in the *New York Times*), he'd dictate his thoughts on a tape recorder, which one of his assistants transcribed and sent to us on bright orange paper, which we irreverently labeled "Orange-Grams." We would cut them down, shape them up, perhaps rearrange the thoughts for clarity, and insert an idea or two that he might have overlooked. Occasionally, if the writers agreed the idea was not one of Chuck's best, the Orange-Gram would quietly disappear. At the next recording session, we'd simply hand him other scripts we thought were better. This strategy of selective amnesia often worked for weeks—and then he would suddenly turn to one of us and say, "Whatever happened to that script about …?" But he was so busy and so prolific that he often forgot about many of his script ideas or simply wanted to move on to a "new idee-er," as he put it in his Boston accent.

It wasn't unusual for Chuck to want a script *right now*—unless he changed his mind, of course. My colleague Roberto Rivera complained, only half-jokingly, that Chuck had given him attention deficit disorder with his habit of asking for a particular script and then calling back an hour later to say, "Stop working on that script and send me this script instead. Right away!"

During the years I was managing editor of *BreakPoint*, Chuck would occasionally call me at home to dictate something straight out of that afternoon's news reports—something he wanted to broadcast the following day. This meant I sometimes had to compose a script for him in less than an hour to make the early evening recording deadline, fending off my children's complaints that they were hungry, and when were we going to have dinner?

Several of his writers worked for Chuck for so long that we knew exactly what he would want to say about a particular issue—he was, after all, a good teacher. But one of my colleagues told me it was a bit creepy that I could even insert Chuck's ad-libs for him.

Over the years, we tried hard to draw Chuck away from politically oriented scripts to do more worldview-related scripts on art, music, and science. But he loved politics and found it hard to resist the temptation to comment on everything going on in Washington.

Chuck was well aware of his audience's quirks. Some years ago he asked his writers to pull together a list of great films for his listening audience. Knowing how much he'd loved the recently released *Saving Private Ryan*, I added it to the list. When Chuck went over the list at the next editorial meeting, he turned to me in mock horror, his eyes twinkling. "Anne! I can't have R-rated movies on my list! I'm a famous evangelical!" He knew perfectly well that, were he to include any R-rated films, no matter how excellent the content, he would receive letters of complaint from overly sensitive listeners who seemed unable to look any further than a film's rating.

Chuck loved to tease people, and some of his pranks were legendary. I had a taste of his sense of humor a few years ago when I applied for a job requiring a background check. Chuck called me up one day to tell me that the FBI had informed him that their investigation of me had uncovered something pretty serious, and that because of it, I would not get the job. I was so stunned I couldn't speak. And then I heard laughter coming down the telephone line. Just one of his little jokes.

Chuck often opened meetings with a story about someone he encountered in his travels around the world who told him how much he had learned from *BreakPoint*. I think it was comments like these that kept him going, although a daily radio program was difficult, given his heavy schedule. As for me, after nearly two decades and hundreds of scripts, I still became absurdly pleased when I heard that Chuck had particularly liked something I wrote.

While Chuck's big focus in *BreakPoint* was teaching worldview, he never tired of finding new ways to explain the faith that had changed the life of this Watergate felon forever. What follows are his thoughts, previously unpublished, on some of the subjects that concerned him most. Rereading them, I was struck by how prophetic his insights proved to be. And I could almost hear his voice as I read them.

Chuck had a fertile mind, and he was constantly generating ideas and sending them to his writers. He never stopped thinking about what was going on in the world, good or bad, and how Christians should respond to these events. He would even get out of his pool, where he took a daily swim, to grab his tape recorder and dictate his thoughts lest he forget them.

This habit of constant thinking meant we had far more memos than we could possibly turn into columns or *BreakPoint* commentaries. The good news is, we have enough of these "leftover" memos to fill an entire book—the one you are about to read.

My thanks to the *BreakPoint* team for providing me access to Chuck's memos. A special thanks to Chuck's assistant, Sherrie Irvin, for the many hours she spent finding, organizing, and getting to me hundreds and hundreds of these memos. Thanks as well to *BreakPoint* editor David Carlson—to whom many of these memos were addressed; to Colson Center Vice-President Steve Bradford; and to my friend Kim Moreland, whose memory and researching skills proved invaluable.

For readability, I shortened the longer pieces and made some minor alterations. In addition, where necessary I have provided an introduction to the subject, indicated in italics. However, the memos that follow are vintage Chuck. I hope you will enjoy reading them as much as we did.

Anne Morse

November 2014

# 1

# APOLOGETICS

# The Question of Sin

The one thing a secular worldview can never pro-
vide is an answer to guilt and sin. Nor can it form the basis for
reconciliation.

In fact, nothing apart from Judeo-Christian revelation can provide a basis for restoring a community that has been torn apart
by sin—or offer hope of forgiveness and restoration to those who
are burdened by sin. I have discovered while preaching in Hindu
and Buddhist cultures that whenever I talk about forgiveness and
a new life in Christ, eyes just bulge. This is something people
haven't heard.

I remember in the Trevandrum prison in India, a thousand
inmates looked up at me—outcasts, doomed to live with their sin
for the rest of their lives, and then to have done to them in the next
life what they did to someone in this life, which simply perpetu-
ates evil. I told them they could be forgiven, that Christ died on
the cross for their sins. The response was absolutely staggering.

I also remember the time I was in Japan, and met with a professor of comparative religion at the University of Yokohama. He
was a Buddhist, of course, and had studied *Born Again* and used it
as a textbook in his class on the Christian religion. He had asked
to meet with me. We had a great conversation. I talked about forgiveness in the prisons and asked him how Buddhists could provide for forgiveness since there was no redemption, no Savior;
no one had died for their sins. He said they had a new form of
Buddhism called Pure Land Buddhism, where they can provide a
level of forgiveness in the next life.

Buddhism, of course, is infinitely flexible; there is no one true
God. There are simply stages of consciousness, and so to solve
a dilemma—my question was how do you preach Buddhism
in a prison—they simply invent a new sect or strain of belief to
accommodate a particular need. It's almost amusing, but it also
shows how bankrupt the system is.

Most secular thought today is parallel to Buddhism. It's really the same thing. We don't have a God in the secular world today, so we simply develop states of consciousness. We get in touch with our own feelings. We seek a higher state of consciousness or peace with nature.

How do you deal with the question of sin once you're aware of it? You can develop some better way to get in touch with your feelings and improve your self-esteem, but it won't solve the problem because the consequences of that guilt are there. You can't get rid of them. You can go to psychologists and they can try to help you get rid of the repressed memories and do all sorts of therapeutic gymnastics, but they can't get to the heart of the problem.

Only Christianity provides for that forgiveness and the subsequent healing that can take place in the individual's life and in the community. Kim Phuc, the little Vietnamese girl who became famous through a photograph showing her running naked after being burned by napalm, demonstrates this. If out of the horrors of war a young girl hideously burned can forgive those who dropped the bombs on her, then there is hope that the cycle of evil can be broken, guilt can be released, and people can be freed from bondage. This really is overcoming evil with good (Romans 12:21). There is no other way. Every secular system is doomed, as is Buddhism, as is Hinduism, as is Islam. It is only Jews and Christians who have a way out, and only the Christian has a way out by the grace of God.

This is an incredibly important and powerful apologetic.

# Thank God for Peter Singer

I gave a lecture at Gordon-Conwell Theological Seminary titled "Thank God for Peter Singer." The thesis is that when you want to make an apologetic argument, the best thing you can do is to force your adversaries to embrace the logical conclusion of their own ideas.

I mentioned a little story about my recent discussion with an agnostic, which illustrates my point. I forced this man to take his statement that all religions are alike, and reconcile it with the exclusive truth claims of Christianity. I said all religions can't be alike; they can't all lead to the same place because Christianity specifically denies that. So if all religions are equally true, then Christianity's truth nullifies the other religions.

I then got into a discussion of the law of noncontradiction, and drove him into a corner where he eventually had no choice but to say, "I have to admit that some things are extra natural." He wouldn't agree to supernatural, but he did have to conclude extra, at which point I said, "Precisely." He could not defend a naturalistic explanation for his own proposition.

That's the most effective apologetic there is.

# The Question of God

I am two-thirds of the way through Armand Nicholi's book *The Question of God*, which contrasts the teachings of Sigmund Freud and C. S. Lewis. It is filled with wonderful apologetics.

For example, it's extremely useful to understand the role of the superego in terms of conscience in Freud's analysis. Freud has substituted the superego for God; if your conscience is being informed, it is being informed by the superego. Well, superego is just a made-up name. There's no more scientific validity to that than there is in saying God speaks to you.

Nicholi's comparison of Freud's view on natural law and C. S. Lewis's was also brilliantly done. Even though you're getting an objective presentation of both viewpoints, readers will come away with a realization that Lewis's position is vastly superior, because we know within ourselves what is right or wrong. Everybody does. So has the superego been taught, character passed on from our earthly father, father to son? If so, how did the first father come to know what is right and wrong? He didn't have any father to pass anything on to him.

Freud's arguments just blow away in the breeze as you read this book. It's absolutely brilliant.

*The Question of God* is Comparative Worldview 101, built around two great minds. Armand also weaves the gospel in, telling the story of Lewis's transformation, and points out that Freud actually admired religious people.

Armand finds inconsistencies in Freud's statements, though he doesn't say that. For instance, Freud talks about the importance of moral law as if there were a moral law.

This is apologetics in its most important form.


# Idolatry Alongside

While Moses is up on the mountain for forty days talking to the Lord and receiving the Ten Commandments, the people below start grumbling. Gathering around Aaron, they said, "Come, make us gods who will go before us." And then, dismissively, they add, "As for this fellow Moses who brought us out of Egypt, we don't know what has happened to him" (Exodus 32:1).

Notice how, in appealing to Aaron, the Israelites put down Moses as his competitor. In effect they say, "We don't know where this guy's gone. He's up mountain climbing, and we're trying to get on our way here and be delivered."

Aaron, in turn, told them to take off their gold earrings. He melted down the gold, and "made it into an idol cast in the shape of a calf, fashioning it with a tool. Then they said, 'These are your gods, Israel, who brought you up out of Egypt'" (Exodus 32:4).

But note what it says in verse 5: "When Aaron saw this, he built an altar in front of the calf and announced, 'Tomorrow there will be a festival to the Lord.'"

Theologian Cornelius Plantinga says this is the classic example of "idolatry alongside."

We tend to think of idolatry as worshiping something other than God. But here we have a scene of two altars, one the golden calf, and the other the altar to God, side by side, and you could take your pick. But people wouldn't take their pick, of course; they worshiped both. It's sort of like hedging your bets, I suppose, or having your cake and eating it too. Because it means at one level you can worship God and at another level you can worship mammon.

And this is what all of us do.

Yes, we worship the Lord our God with all our heart, mind, and soul—but not exclusively. We also worship a lot of other things in life, including our reputation, our money, our family, and our dreams for our kids. None of these things are bad in and of themselves. But the reality is that, taken too far, it's "idolatry alongside."

Luther also made this point. He argued that idolatry wasn't simply worshiping something other than God; it was worshiping something alongside God, and this is much more typical of the human condition.

Plantinga offers an interesting parallel. Idolatry and adultery go alongside each other in the Bible. Think about a middle-aged, married man who starts an affair with another woman. It isn't that he doesn't love the other woman: he does. It's that he tries to love both his wife and the other woman. This is a direct parallel with what people do with idolatry.

Of course, as the man discovers, you can't continue to love both unless you live a dual life, and after a while, that is completely destructive, as I've seen in the lives of so many people. So you ultimately have to make a choice: Which one do you love more?

The problem with adultery is that when you make the choice to commit it, you break your covenant with God in the first relationship; you have made the decision to worship something else. So there is a parallel between adultery and idolatry.

This is a very sobering, jolting understanding of idolatry. Throw into the mix here Calvin's belief that we are incorrigibly religious—that is, we are made in such a way that we cannot avoid worshiping something or someone. The reason we can't, I believe, is that we're made in the image of God. We know we have not created ourselves; therefore, there is a Creator, or some god, small "g" or big "g," that we are driven to worship. We can't be at peace until we do.

With adultery, people are forced to face the compartmentalization of their lives; they know they are living a lie.

But with "idolatry alongside," they're not. Many of us go blissfully through life, worshiping both God and something else—a basic flaw in Christian discipleship.

Getting back to Moses and Aaron, there's a humorous scene later in Exodus 32, when Moses comes down from the mountain and sees what the Israelites have been up to in his absence. He's furious! He smashes the tablets, burns the golden calf, and says to Aaron, "What did these people do to you that you led them into such great sin?" (Exodus 32:21).

Aaron's answer is absolutely classic. "Do not be angry, my Lord.... You know how prone these people are to evil" (v. 22). (Notice how he shifts the blame onto the people.)

Then he repeats what the people said to him, and explains that he told them to take off their gold jewelry and throw it in the fire. He then says, "And out came this calf!" (v. 24), as if they had simply thrown the gold on the fire and presto! Out came a calf.

So here's Aaron, lying to Moses, who has just been with God.

The ancient Israelites—like us—were incorrigible. And of course, the Lord brought great judgment upon them for their idolatry.

The point is, we're going to worship something, so if we don't worship the one true God, we'll start worshiping nature, ourselves, money, or something else. But we will worship something.

# Something to Cling To

During my devotions today I started trying to imagine God and found it impossible to do so. You can only think of Him as the all-powerful, omniscient Creator. But you can't imagine what He looks like.

God is outside of time and space. He is therefore beyond human comprehension. This is terribly scary when you think about it, because when we die we're going somewhere. Heaven is described to us figuratively in Scripture, but with our finite minds, we have no way of comprehending what it will be like, what we will be conscious of, what we'll remember from the past, or what we'll know. But we do know we'll be in a different dimension, which is a very awesome thought. It's a little bit like the film *The Truman Show*, where the character named Truman discovers he's been living on a stage all his life, and when he walks through a door in the sky, he's finally into reality.

For us, heavenly reality is going to be even more difficult to comprehend because it is very likely going to be totally unlike any human experience, so we'll have nothing to gauge it by. There is nothing, as we sit and contemplate now, that we can fix our minds upon.

We don't know (apart from Christ, of course) whether we'll be in a state of continual bliss or continuous pain. We don't know whether we'll be ascending into the clouds, with the glorious images that conjures up, or descending into the abyss. No amount of human reason can get us over this obstacle, this lack of comprehension.

So in one sense we're utterly helpless, alone in the cosmos with no idea of where we're going to land, what it will be like, what our experiences will be, or what God will be like. We can, as I believe, know intellectually that there is a God — that creation is inexplicable any other way. We can know God by experiencing Him in our lives, and we can sense and see His power (as we read in Romans 1 and 2), but we can't grasp it with our finite minds. This creates a terrible sense of alienation and frustration, particularly as you get older and realize that the day of judgment, when you leave this earth and your soul goes somewhere else, is humanly unfathomable.

So what can we cling to? The human Jesus.

I think this is one of the many reasons that God sent His only begotten Son to earth: So that we could have Someone who would lead us, who was going ahead of us to prepare the way. Someone we would know and be able to identify with in some ways. Someone who experienced what we have experienced and who has gone on before us.

So just when your spiritual life seems bleakest, when you're grasping, struggling, clawing for some understanding of God and what lies beyond in eternity, and you come to the point of utter frustration, picture Jesus—warm and friendly, cooking fish with His disciples by the lakeside, walking with them down the paths, and sitting around the table.

This is the context in which we think of Jesus. And we suddenly have something to cling to, which is a picture of what lies beyond. Without Christ, we would be like Charlie Chaplin, who, when he was told no life had been discovered in the universe, said, "I feel lonely."

The more intimate we are with Jesus, the more assured we are of what lies ahead. The closer I fellowship with Him, the stronger my assurance and comfort regarding the future. Without that relationship with Jesus, one would approach the end of one's life with enormous trepidation.

Following this realization, I had a long conversation with Bill Bright, who is dying and knows it. He has probably a matter of months to live, but is in the most joyous state he has ever been in. He told me that this year, since he learned he did not have long to live, has been the most productive one of his life. He has produced a series of books, won an award for one of them, and is presently working on many other books and pamphlets.

Bill told me excitedly about the book he has almost finished. It is on Jesus—his intimate, personal relationship with Jesus, and why it is so important to share Him with others. How Jesus has become so close to him in his last months on earth. Bill told me that, as he has approached death, he has felt a deepening appreciation of the person of Jesus. And he's had a deepening desire to share with others that intimate relationship with Christ.

The Christian life indeed starts with Jesus and ends with Him.

He is the Alpha and Omega. Without Him, the physical Jesus, we would have nothing but the promises written in a book. We would be traveling into some distant place or state of being beyond human comprehension, and we would be traveling alone. Even if we believed God's promises fully as related in the Scriptures, it would still be bone-chilling. But we have the ultimate comfort of knowing that we'll be taken by the hand of the Jesus we know and can understand and experience.

# Attacks on Truth

*In the final years of his life, Chuck spoke out a great deal about the increasing attacks on public expressions of faith and the need for Christians to refuse to buckle under attempts to force them to keep silent about their beliefs — or worse, attempts to force them to deny those beliefs. He saw clearly that a key apologetic task was defending a place for public expressions of the faith.*

It is absolutely amazing what a lightning rod Justice Antonin Scalia is for the press. Some years ago, when he talked about believing in the resurrection, he was pilloried by the Washington press corps. *Washington Post* columnist Richard Cohen even suggested Scalia wasn't fit to serve on the court. In the *New York Times*, Sean Wilentz jumped all over Scalia for talking about government being ordained of God, something believed by many Jews and Christians. What it comes down to is, Wilentz was attacking Scalia for the fact that he is a Christian who takes seriously what he believes.

If we follow Wilentz's reasoning, it would be impossible for anyone who is a serious believer to serve in public office. This would constitute a religious test; Scalia is accused of threatening democracy. That's a pretty serious charge.

People have to understand that this isn't just an attack on Scalia; it's a serious attack on any truth claim. In other words, if people like Scalia or Clarence Thomas take seriously their faith, then by definition they're disqualified. The only way people of faith could get by the kind of objections Wilentz raised would be to denounce their own faith. In other words, to keep quiet about what they really believe. In effect, they would have to be stealth Christians or Jews.

I don't think people like Wilentz really understand what they're doing. Scalia's truth claim was reduced to "private prejudices." In reality, a truth claim is an expression of one's deepest beliefs. The attack in this case is clearly upon truth, which is at the heart of the conflict of worldviews.

What Scalia's critics are really after is preventing Christians from expressing truth claims in public. That's where we're going to see the real anti-Christian bias over the next few years. I hesitate to call it anti-Christian bias, however, because in a sense it isn't: it's an anti-truth bias. It's a demand that all truth claims be reduced to nothing more than personal opinions—but then, of course, they're not truth claims.

# The Key in the Lock

G. K. Chesterton makes an incredible argument in *Orthodoxy*, particularly when he considers the paradoxes of Christianity. He says, "And it did for one wild moment cross my mind that perhaps those [the agnostics and critics and skeptics] might not be the very best judges of the relation of religion to happiness, who by their own account had neither one nor the other."[1]

What he is highlighting, of course, is that non-Christians, particularly those hostile to the faith, preach a message of despair. They cannot have any *telos*, any goal or purpose or hope in life other than the satisfactions of the moment, which are not very satisfying.

Chesterton makes the point elsewhere that we're not really content in this world because, as C. S. Lewis also argues, we know we're made for something else. So why should we be listening to people who have no religion and have no happiness when they preach to us about religion and happiness? They've abandoned the search.

Chesterton also makes the argument that Christian creeds precisely fit the complexity of the world in the way that they unlock the door to what the world is. He argues that Christian creeds are complex and difficult to understand and sometimes contradictory. True. And then he talks about the ambiguities and paradoxes of the world. But he says that, as he examines them, that they are like a key in a lock: "But a key and a lock are both complex. And if a key fits a lock, you know it is the right key."[2]

What a brilliant analogy! Christianity is the complex key that unlocks the mysteries of the world. This is how, in the crucible of his own experiences and in his relaying his case for orthodoxy, Chesterton comes to realize that Christianity is exactly what it purports to be. It is about discovering reality in the world.

Finally, Chesterton writes that the critics are so eager to denounce Christianity that they contradict one another. Some criticize Christianity because it is one thing; others criticize it because it is precisely the opposite thing. As he put it, "What again could this astonishing thing be like, which people are so anxious to contradict, that in doing so they did not mind contradicting themselves?"[3] He really makes the case that because people are so overly zealous to denounce Christianity, there must be something to it. And that the case they're denouncing seems to have more sense than the manner and style and content of their denunciations.

This is exactly the case with Russian dissident and poet Irina Ratushinskaya, who became a Christian through the "witness" of the Communists. They tried so hard to tell her there wasn't any God that she came to realize that there must be one. If there were no God, why were they trying so hard to destroy faith in Him? Great argument.

The other powerful theme that runs throughout Chesterton's *Orthodoxy* is this: Everything that Chesterton is discovering about human nature and life and the world is what was already discovered long before by Christianity. He likens himself to a man who is on a great adventuresome voyage to a distant continent. And when he lands on the continent, he comes off the ship—and discovers he's in England, where he started. He finds nothing on his voyage that he did not already know.

What Chesterton is saying is that we already know Christianity is true, and the more we explore belief systems, the more we come back to what we've been told is true. In other words, Christianity is real, not because of anything we discover, but because in the process of our discovery and in our probing for other things, we come back to the one truth that has already been discovered for us.

This is the basis of orthodoxy—that is, it is unchanging. It is not one thing in one age and another thing in a different age.

# The Offense of the Gospel

During our quiet time this morning, my wife Patty and I read Acts 17. I was reminded that Paul, both in Thessalonica and Athens, "reasoned" with the Jews and the Greeks, as Acts records, "explaining and proving that the Messiah had to suffer and rise from the dead" (v. 3).

What Paul was doing was explaining the gospel. The reason he had to do that at Thessalonica is because they had never heard it before. Same thing in Athens.

My contention is we live in a postmodern culture which has lost any sense of biblical literacy—which believes that truth is negotiable, a mere personal preference. It's a culture that has no concept of its own sin. So before we can really present the good news that Jesus died for our sins, we have to reason and explain, as Paul did. People need to be led through a line of reasoning that leads them to the conclusion that God is and must be, and that you can know this God.

Notice, also, that the Jews of Thessalonica were furious. "They dragged Jason and some other brothers before the city officials, shouting: 'These men who have caused trouble all over the world have now come here, and Jason has welcomed them into his house. They are all defying Caesar's decrees, saying that there is another king, one called Jesus' " (Acts 17:6–7).

What is the offense of the gospel? Another king—and it has been this way all through the centuries. This explains the resistance of American intellectuals and the cultural elite to the gospel: We are proclaiming another loyalty. When we teach Intelligent Design, for example, we are teaching our kids that there is a higher power to which they are beholden. What does that do to the authority of their teacher, principal, or textbook writer, or other cultural elites who think they really do run the world? To them, Christians are "causing trouble all over the world." But it's inherent in the nature of our message.

That's what's so clear here in Acts. The persecution that Paul, Silas, and others experienced is no different from what many people are experiencing around the world today. Most of us in the West aren't beaten or stoned—at least, not physically. But we take plenty of hate. Look at the recent *Washington Post* review of Jonathan Aitken's book *Pride and Perjury*. It was pure slander. What was Jonathan's offense? The gospel.

When Paul fled to Athens, he apparently waited there alone, and was bothered to see that the city was full of idols. He reasoned in the synagogue with the Jews and the god-fearing Greeks, and also spoke in the marketplace, day by day, with those who happened to be there. Among these were Epicureans (people who believed hedonism was the purpose of life) and Stoics (who believed that you should just endure anything—that life is nasty, brutish, and short).

The people complained, and brought Paul to a meeting at the Areopagus. They were curious. I sense from Luke's account of this event that they were the kind of people who just lived for and off ideas. They were the coffeehouse dreamers; as Luke expresses it in verse 21: "All the Athenians and the foreigners who lived there spent their time doing nothing but talking about and listening to the latest ideas." This was the Greenwich Village crowd, or the denizens of the Left Bank in Paris.

In the middle of this Mars Hill crowd, Paul delivered his incredible sermon. What is particularly significant about the sermon is that Paul picked out one of the Greeks' cultural icons—the altar to an unknown God. He told them he was going to explain to them who this unknown God was.

This is classic apologetics. This is what we do on *BreakPoint*. We take a film such as *The Matrix*, for instance, critique it, and ask, "What is this film really saying to you? What philosophy is the director promulgating?"

This is what a missionary to an unreached culture must do.

As you follow Paul's strategy you see the perfect template for a strategy today in a culture—ours—which is as foreign to the good news in many ways as Athens was then.

As Paul finished up, note that many sneered at him. But a few men became followers: Dionysius, a woman named Demaris, and a number of others.

I've been to Mars Hill, which is just down the mountain slightly from the Acropolis. It's interesting that on Good Friday, at noon, the flag at the Acropolis is lowered to half-staff, and on Easter Sunday morning, the resurrection, the flag is raised to full staff.

So what is the message of Mars Hill? Paul goes in, reasons, argues, uses apologetics, and challenges them with the faith. Only a few follow. But two thousand years later, in that great worldwide symbol of Greek culture and the glory of Athens, the flag is raised on Easter Sunday morning.

Christianity cannot be stopped ... because it is true.

# Sawing Off the Branch

*In this memo, Chuck tackles the Age of Reason, why it failed, and — yes, there's an apologetic point here — why revelation and reason need each other.*

I recently listened to the seventh tape in a series by Vishal Mangalwadi. He makes an interesting point that I want to get rooted in my thoughts. The explanation for why the Age of Reason failed is that it divorced itself from revelation. It said that we could know anything and everything ultimately by reason.

The problem is that reason alone cannot give us ultimate conclusions.

Mangalwadi illustrates this well by pointing out that Aristotle assumes the eternal existence of the universe. But that is not a testable assumption; it requires faith.

The Christians came along and gave a basis for the eternal existence of the universe: faith. In the logocentric universe, God created us and spoke us into being, and therefore gave a basis for logic (logos).

So from the time of the introduction of the Judeo-Christian tradition, you had a fundamental premise on which all logic rested; that is, God is, and He has spoken. But in the Age of Reason, the Enlightenment, we took away that premise, believing that we could know everything by reason. This was a return to a pure Aristotelian argument.

And of course it collapsed, because in the Age of Reason, we discovered that by reason alone you could not prove the existence of God. But the existence of God, of course, was necessary as the first foundation from which reason proceeds. So in the Age of Reason we sawed off the branch we were sitting on. Reason unsupported by revelation could not survive.

The death of God, therefore, spelled the death of reason, because it took away the fundamental premise on which our pursuit of reason rested. So in the modern era we discovered the limits of reason — and in the process had nowhere to turn.

Postmodernism is simply an attack on the logocentric universe. In fact, that's how deconstruction got started. Obviously, without God, logocentrism collapses. So postmodernism becomes simply the vacuum. What is there after you dispense with reason? Nothing but despair and cynicism.

The supreme irony is that faith, which regarded the Age of Reason as an assault on faith, is, it turns out, essential to the survival of reason. And the Age of Reason, which attacked God, undermined its own premises. The conclusion, of course, is that reason and revelation need one another. You cannot understand all of life without using reason. Reason is made possible by revelation. The only hope is the rescue of reason by reintroducing revelation into the formation of modern thought.

# Lost in the Cosmos

*Can the truth be known apart from Scripture? Yes. In this section Chuck argues that we can use the truths found in nature to point unbelievers to the truth of the gospel and God's teachings about how we are to live our lives.*

I had an excellent conversation once with R. C. Sproul on the question of natural theology. Jonathan Edwards was strongly into natural theology — that is, that the truth can be known apart from Scripture. It can be known from general revelation. It can be known from observing things which Scripture doesn't even deal with. The fundamental operative argument here is that all truth is God's truth.

Thomas Aquinas was confronted with a huge problem along these lines: Islamic scholars of his day, when Islam was a shining light of culture, argued that there was such a thing as double truth — that is, something could be true in science but not in faith.

Aquinas took issue with this. He said there was only one certain truth. He got into the question of how things were knowable, and he said, "Some things are knowable by nature; some things are knowable by grace" — just exactly what I believe and what natural theology teaches.

Evangelical scholars such as Francis Schaeffer have generally shied away from Aquinas because they believe he is separating truth into two kinds of truth — truth that you get from grace and truth that you get from science or nature. But they're ignoring the fact that Aquinas also said there are some truths, like the truth about God, that are known by both nature and grace.

In the final analysis, in any event, all truth comes from both. There is a unity of truth; it all comes from God. Aquinas, according to Sproul, was not separating nature and grace. He was simply trying to demonstrate what was false about the Muslim worldview and certain Aristotelian formulations that Muslim scholars had come up with.

The fact of the matter is, I believe, that truth is knowable both by revelation and by nature. And the reason I believe this is that it is often the same thing: revelation tells us about the creation, but the creation is just as knowable by our physical senses as it is by Scripture. All Scripture is doing is telling us that truth is knowable by creation because it refers to creation in the mountains, which declare the glory of God.

The Scriptures, as well, are historically recounting the actions of God working among His covenant people and the nations of history. Scripture doesn't make God's actions true; the Scripture itself is validating what actually happened, which was the source of the truth, God's actions in the lives of people.

Similarly, the Epistles are written by men under the influence of the Holy Spirit. They are without error, yet the truth is not necessarily what is told us propositionally (though it is the truth). The Scripture is describing moral truth, which God has wired into the universe and revealed to the writer. When you trace these things back, they all go back to God. The Scripture is truth, but it is also describing truth.

Now the problem, of course, comes when people believe that this opens the door to rationalism. Now, there's nothing wrong with being rational; the problem is attaching the "ism" to it. In a sense one is indeed attaching the "ism" if one were to argue that everything is knowable apart from God, and with one's own mind one could come to moral formulations and understand the moral laws of the universe as one can the physical law: by observation. Therefore, one doesn't need the Scripture, and therefore, one reduces God to the force that started it all and wound it up and created it; that's how one becomes a Deist.

But I would never suggest anyone could be saved by any revelation apart from the truth of the Scripture itself. Common grace can be understood rationally, but saving knowledge means that Christ, who died on the cross—and again, the gospel, which is presented as a description of that truth—is revealed through Scripture. You have to hear the good news presented from Scripture; you have to have the gift of faith given to you by God. You have to, with that faith, react and be declared righteous. That's the process of salvation. Human beings cannot do this. You can't get there from here.

But there is a unity of truth even with regard to the good news, which rests on historical events. Christianity is, after all, a religion of history, so why would one exclude sources of understanding truth? If you were to carry this too far, you would say that God spoke once and for all through Scripture; He could never reveal anything again. And yet, there are continuous revelations out of nature.

Remember, too, the story of Nein Cheng, who was put into prison during China's Cultural Revolution. She had only the sayings of Chairman Mao's little red book. She was not allowed a Bible, but she looked up one day and saw a spider weaving a web, and she suddenly saw the hand of God in the beauty of the design. (What makes this particularly telling is that Jonathan Edwards also believed that the spiderweb was one of God's great architectural creations.) Now, here comes this spider into a jail cell where a woman is languishing with her hands bound behind her, and she sees God in this spider; she is spiritually renewed. Did she not see the truth? Of course she saw the truth. That spiderweb was her Bible.

We are crazy when we say that all truth can only be known by Scripture; that becomes a circular argument. God says you cannot add to or subtract from Scripture, but nowhere does the Bible tell us that this is the complete source of all truth. It *is* a complete source of all truth—for salvation—but not for other considerations. We have to be able to look at nature's revelation, as well.

The interesting thing about this whole exercise is that I came to these thoughts on my own. I did not read a book about Thomist points of view and then react. I did not listen to a great debate over presuppositional apologetics. I was just thinking deeply about these issues and came out at a point where, lo and behold, I discovered I was embracing arguments made by Aquinas without even realizing it. In fact, I got into natural law arguments over the homosexuality issue. Until I started discussing these arguments with *BreakPoint* writer Roberto Rivera, I'm sorry to confess, I didn't even realize they were Thomist arguments.

To me this makes so much sense that I don't know how you can argue about it. There is truth; there is reality. The ultimate reality has to be in the first cause. What started everything? By whom, through whom, and for whom all things were made has to be the beginning. There is one ultimate truth that holds together everything that exists.

By definition, that is God. We know it by faith because Christ came and revealed Himself, and we believe in Him and have come to that faith. We can see the truth of that faith in the creation around us and in the Scriptures. But even somebody who wasn't a believer would know that there's got to be some source of ultimate truth. We can't always have just been here. An infinite universe begs the question. So once you get to the first-cause question, you get to the proposition that there has to be a God, and then you have to look at history. You have to begin to probe the truth. Where do you find truth? Were the Islamic scholars right in the thirteenth century? Let's look at their proposition. They did not work out very well. How did the various political systems founded on differing presuppositions work out? Some have survived better than others.

I believe we are given, by God, certain abilities, and we're to use those abilities to understand reality. And God has made certain things that make ultimate reality clear to us. Nature is one of them; Paul says so in Romans 2. He says here too there is a truth that is built within us. But we also know that from experience. The Tao is an example. Where does wisdom come from? It comes from God; all truth is from God.

I can see the vulnerability of this argument because it could clearly lead you away from Scripture unless you keep as your presupposition that Scripture is true. And why do we believe it?

Because we believe God wrote the Bible, and it has been proven over the years to be infallible, and because it says it's true on its face.

"Your [God's] word is truth," Jesus says (John 17:17). So we accept that presupposition, but we do not close our minds to other forms of inquiry that will enable us to defend the reality reflected in truth wherever we find it. God speaks it in one form, and He displays it in many other forms. Are we now separating nature and grace? Not at all. We're saying they are complementary.

The only thing that makes life meaningful is if it is tied to truth—otherwise we are adrift in the cosmos; we are lost. We will drift around looking for some place to moor the boat. We'll be caught up in the fads of the moment, and living with false presuppositions. So the most urgent, the most desperate need is to find truth.

So we have to be rooted in truth. That truth is then going to lead us to certain propositions that will give us a meaningful and fulfilling life.

# 2

# BIOETHICS
## and LIFE ISSUES

# A Principled Stand

The East Room of the White House was packed. As I sat listening to President George W. Bush, my spine tingled. I had frankly thought America was so far down the road in its post-Christian journey that I would never again hear a president of the United States make a principled moral statement, speak about ethics plainly, and indeed, mark a line in the sand, saying, "Beyond this moral barrier we will not move."

But as I looked around the room, my spine tingled for yet another reason. Across the aisle was seated a bearded Christian theologian, Nigel Cameron. I first met Nigel when he was just out of seminary and working in Edinburgh, Scotland, running a place called Rutherford House. He was a bright young Christian scholar. We got to be friends, and I discovered he had a passion for the bioethics questions. This was decades ago, when nobody was even thinking about bioethics. Over coffee at Rutherford House, Nigel told me that he saw bioethics as the dominant issue in the years ahead, and explained why. He was so impassioned about the issue that he had helped start a journal on bioethics in London, the first of its kind. A sentry on the front lines for the church, he saw this issue coming, and he began to educate himself and others on the many ramifications, the grave dangers of what C. S. Lewis called "The Abolition of Man."

Over the years, Nigel and I stayed in touch. I appreciated his effort and supported it, although I found it was getting very little reception in the Christian world. When people talked of life issues, they thought only of abortion. Nigel was concerned about abortion, but he also saw "life issues" in terms of creating life in a test tube, with far-reaching implications for humanity.

Nigel eventually became dean of the Wilberforce Forum, and soon laid the cloning issue down as primary. He began working with others to build a coalition.

Looking around the East Room yesterday, I realized that most of the guests were part of Nigel's coalition, energized by Nigel. I thought to myself that one person *can* make a difference. If we really are determined, if we really are following God's will, then we're never outnumbered. God is sovereign, and He works through His people in the most amazing ways. There must have been times over the last fifteen or twenty years when Nigel wondered if he could get anyone interested in bioethics issues, and if he could ever make a difference. And yet there he was, a Scotsman, now a naturalized American citizen, sitting in the White House listening to the president of the United States, the most powerful man in the world, eloquently making the very arguments Nigel had been expounding over the years.

Directly in front of me was another amazing person, sitting in her wheelchair: Joni Eareckson Tada. A diving accident when she was a teenager left Joni a quadriplegic, and she illustrates, as Nigel does, what one person totally committed to Him can do. Joni sat there as the Christian answer to Christopher Reeve, another quadriplegic, but unlike Reeve, Joni opposed any effort to destroy human life in order to advance her cause and perhaps offer her relief from her disability. Over the years, she must have experienced great discouragement; her chances of having a normal life were gone, and she'd never have the chance to be a mother or grandmother, and yet, her spirit never seemed to weaken.

I've never been with Joni when she didn't lift me up. She has the most beautiful Christlike spirit of anybody I know, and she does day by day what she has to do, faithfully serving God with great energy and enthusiasm. And she ended up sitting directly in front of the podium with the United States president speaking about her. When Bush finished, he came off the platform and went over and immediately embraced her and kissed her on the cheek. For just such a time as this did God allow Joni to go through great pain and suffering and anxiety. But He had a purpose: that she would be available for that very moment to be called before kings and governors and God would give her the words to speak, which indeed He did.

# A Flight to Amsterdam

During a flight from Detroit to Amsterdam, I was impressed by a particularly gracious crew in the business class cabin. One woman, middle-aged, I suppose, was especially helpful. She had a lovely smile no matter what we asked. She offered us things throughout the long flight, and was exceptionally friendly.

As we neared Amsterdam, this crew member, while clearing away our breakfast dishes, asked what we were planning to do in Amsterdam. We told her we were attending the Billy Graham Conference on Evangelism. She asked a number of questions about it, and said she thought it was wonderful. I told her I worked in prison ministry, and she told me that she has spent years singing in a church choir that performed in prisons.

We got into a great conversation about her faith. She was an active Catholic, a regular communicant in her church. She described her home as being an extremely Catholic region of Holland.

Believing by then that I was talking to a Christian, I thought I'd find out what she thought about euthanasia, which, tragically, Holland has become known for. I thought she would find it abhorrent. To my astonishment, she gave me quite an impassioned defense of euthanasia. She said she had seen her own grandmother waste away in agony. Her family wanted to help her die, but before they could arrange it, the grandmother died a natural death. The flight attendant thought it was a wonderful thing that Holland had a system for helping people end their suffering.[1]

I explained to her that suffering could be managed without taking life. In response, she said she had seen everything tried with her grandmother. I asked whether her views were shared by other Christians. She said they were—that they thought it was a wonderfully humane thing because it enabled them to eliminate suffering. She must have used the word *humane* a dozen times.

The woman smiled as she spoke. I decided to find out how far she really would go and how strong her beliefs were. I challenged her with every argument I could think of, including God putting our souls into our bodies when life begins, and that humans cannot make the decision to take life. She countered every argument with pleasant smiles, but she became all the more determined in her beliefs. She said euthanasia was a kind thing, and was absolutely unmoved by any of my arguments.

Then, just as we were about to land, she told me that the important thing is that we should tolerate each other's views. "Respect," she said, "is the ultimate quality. We have to respect each other in our differences." I told her I disagreed with that—that I thought the supreme quality was what Jesus called the two great commandments: To love the Lord our God with all our heart, mind, and soul, and to love our neighbors as ourselves. I told her that if we did that we would truly treat people with godly love and would therefore respect life, even in its extreme last moments.

I didn't dissuade her, and of course, she didn't dissuade me.

What struck me was that here was a Christian, one who appeared to be serious about her beliefs, advocating euthanasia for purely humane reasons. She was smiling the whole time, very gracious. All I could think of was C. S. Lewis's description of the barbarians in our midst not being the Goths and vandals with their clubs climbing over the walls, but the well-dressed people sitting in well-lighted rooms with clean fingernails, deciding what was best for other people.

That is what barbarism really is, inhumanity done in the name of humanity, killing people for their own good.

The crucial question is what happens in a society when the good people—and this woman on the plane was one of the good people—really do believe this. Their views become unshakable; this is what these good people perceive to be the kindest thing they can do. Yet in the name of kindness they perform terrible inhumanity. How do you shake this out of them?

I came away from this chilling encounter gravely concerned because I realized that we're not up against people who decide it's good to get rid of people for expedient reasons, or to cut down medical bills, or because they enjoy killing. In a way, the Nazis were a lot easier to fight than the good people wanting to do "humane" things.

This is a further indication of how the church fails in its mission when it doesn't teach people the hard truths. This pleasant flight attendant, of all people, should have heard from her church what the truth is.

# What Is Normal?

Patty and I sadly had to send our daughter, Emily, and her son, Max, back home to Boston the day before Christmas. Both Patty and I were stricken with the flu, and though we had planned to spend Christmas together, we thought it prudent to get Emily away from the virulent bugs. If she fell ill, who would handle Max?

At the airport waiting for the plane, Emily and I had a conversation that was, for me, an epiphany. We began to talk about Roberto Rivera's memo on eugenics — getting rid of mentally deficient kids. Suddenly I saw something in my daughter that I'd never seen so clearly before: deep convictions.

She talked about her views on partial-birth abortion and why it was so hideous, and how the next step would be [autistic] kids like Max who would be taken. She told me she hoped she could be an influence, reaching others and letting them know how special needs kids like Max, who has a variety of autism, can be the greatest blessing. She looked at me and said, "Daddy, this little boy is God's greatest gift to me. He has taught me how to love and live in ways I never understood before."

I confessed to Emily that for the first two years after Max was born I used to ask God why he gave a child like this to our family. Why couldn't Emily have a perfect kid like everyone else? But now I saw why the Lord had done this: Because Max had totally transformed Emily and had taught us all some marvelous, wonderful lessons. And we've all ended up loving Max more than if he were so-called "normal."

Emily made a couple of fascinating points. First, she said, "What's normal?" Who is to say Max isn't getting more out of life than the kids we call "normal." We had just celebrated Max's birthday at a McDonald's the night before. Both of us had observed that Max had the most fun of any of the kids there, going through the trampolines and slides and toys. Max was literally jumping for joy, smiling and hugging people. Some of the other kids were just sulking through it all.

What's normal? Not a bad question, and one Augustine asked when he saw drunks on the street. He would wonder who was happier: he, the professor of rhetoric, or the drunks.

Emily's second observation was absolutely fascinating. She said you could be in the room with a lot of people, and it was like a blender, everything swirling about nicely. And then Max walks in, and it's like somebody dropped a spoon in the blender; everybody pays attention. Some people are aghast. Some people are loving.

Emily said, "Max forces you to look at yourself and how you look at other people. He's God's way of challenging us in our comforts, making us think of others. He separates people and tells us so much about our own character."

Emily and I then talked about her own growing Christian faith. It's wonderful. Her church has become so important to her. She really believes God has given her a mission of helping people understand kids like Max, and of raising Max to be all that God wants him to be.

Emily also said that she thought perhaps God had brought Max into our family so that I could speak on questions of life with personal authority. Wow!

All I can say is, I drove home without benefit of an automobile. I'm a very lucky dad.

# Who Gets to Live?

I just received a letter from the Death with Dignity Alliance. It was the first time I'd gotten a direct mail piece even remotely like it. The organization was promoting assisted suicide (which quickly becomes euthanasia).

What is so insidious about this is they are obviously mailing it to areas like Naples, Florida, where there are a lot of retired people. Everybody wants to die with dignity. Everybody wants a painless death. Obviously, the answers to this mailing would come back overwhelmingly in support. And people like me, who disagree, aren't going to respond at all. So what they'll get is a loaded reaction. The political Right does this all the time too. I get awful mailings from people wanting money for some cause, and they gear it around a public opinion poll.

What's deadly about the Death with Dignity Alliance's mailing is that it isn't just influencing which candidate a person is going to vote for, or which political party; it is diminishing life—a brilliant, clever, insidious, backdoor way to get people to favor assisted suicide.

The problem is assisted suicide never remains the individual's decision. We have the case of *Compassion in Dying v. State of Washington*, a 120-page opinion handed down by the Ninth Circuit in which the presiding judge in a footnote said, "What do you do with people who can't make the decision themselves; obviously, you make it for them, they're entitled to have it made for them, a constitutional right."[2]

Mercifully, that decision did not get sustained in the Supreme Court, but it's only a matter of time. Sadly, most politicians want to sweep this issue aside because they want to keep their base active, but they also want to get the swing voters.

# A Deadly Trajectory

In the Sunday *New York Times* is an interesting piece entitled "Abortion: Easy Access, Complex Everything Else."[3] Anyone who read this had to come away with the realization that there's something inherently wrong about abortion.

We all know it. Even the women getting abortions. I would suspect even a lot of the people performing them.

The piece was written by Ariel Kaminer, and, as you might expect a writer for the *Times* to do, she talked about how good it is that women can obtain legal abortions. She noted that New York City has the highest number of pregnancies that terminate in abortion—40 percent. It's a figure that should give people shivers. But she addressed it pretty clinically.

Then you read about the doctor who gets his $375, covered mostly by insurance, and who administers an abortifacient drug. He justified it by saying, "I'm old enough to remember pre-*Roe* days ... a little bit of inconvenience for me is nothing compared to what people used to go through."

That's an interesting justification, isn't it? And there's some fascinating stuff about Margaret Sanger and New York being the hotbed of family planning (and eugenics, though the article doesn't mention this).

The part that really gets me is that after twenty weeks, the "women's options narrow," as Kaminer put it. She interviewed a doctor who performs late-term abortions, and this is where the article became truly fascinating.

First of all, the procedure costs $15,000—some of which is covered by insurance. She then went on to describe it as "quite unpleasant." Well, it may be unpleasant for the doctor and the patient, but imagine how it is for the unborn child. It gives me chills.

Dr. Berg, the abortionist, said he tries to avoid getting emotional about his work, but his patients have no such luxury. They end up angry with him, and he said he doesn't understand their anger.

Well, they're angry because this man is about to kill their child, and any woman knows that's wrong. And if you kill what everybody accepts as a human life—that is, after the baby is twenty-four weeks in the womb—and pay $15,000 to kill it, why wouldn't we also kill the Maxes of the world? If you can kill a baby whose body is already mostly outside the mother's body, as is done with partial-birth abortion [illegal in most but not all circumstances in the United States], why not kill babies that are completely born? Princeton's Peter Singer has been advocating this for some time: If you find out something is wrong with a newborn, he argues, you should have a certain time period in which to kill it.

Eric Metaxas wrote about this in his book about Dietrich Bonhoeffer. He describes a Christian community in Germany, called Bethel, for people with epilepsy. By 1900, Bethel was caring for 1,600 disabled persons. Bethel was, as Eric writes, the antithesis of the Nietzschean worldview, which exalts power and strength. These were people with disabilities.

Bonhoeffer visited the community and was deeply impressed. He wrote his grandmother about it. But even at the time of his visit, the Nazi regime was moving toward the legal murder of these people. They were categorized as unfit (shades of Darwin). Eric writes that at this point the Nazis were describing people with disabilities as "useless eaters" who were "unworthy of life."

As Bonhoeffer wrote to his grandmother: "It is sheer madness, as some believe today, that the sick can or ought to be legally eliminated. It is virtually the same as building a tower of Babel, and is bound to avenge itself."[4] What a statement. In August 1933, Eric writes, the community was an "oasis of peace, and a living testament to the best of true German Christian culture."[5] But only shortly after that time those very people were taken; they disappeared.

This is a very strong point which illustrates how fast the culture can change. German Christian culture had some of the world's greatest theologians and finest scientific minds. But in a five-year period it went from protecting the helpless to killing them. It's astonishing. And the church didn't pay much attention. All through Eric's book you see how frustrated Bonhoeffer was by the weakness of the church and its unwillingness to take a stand. I mean, it is just astonishing.

So what would happen in America if suddenly we really had the economic crisis that many of us fear is lurking around the corner if we do not start cutting expenditures dramatically? What would happen is that the Maxes of the world, who are costing a lot of money to maintain, would be gone. And there would be some of us who would be screaming and standing in the way, but that wouldn't stop it, any more than the Germans stopped it.

The story of Nazi Germany is really the story of the weakness of human beings, the fallen nature, of how easily — under the exigencies of the moment — we succumb to the worst kinds of evils. I know nobody likes drawing comparisons with the Nazis, and I understand why. There's nothing going on in American life today that even begins to approach what was happening under the Nazis. But eugenics is back, as Dr. Christopher Hook of the Mayo Clinic has said. And it's like a time bomb ticking. You look at the events of the thirties, and you realize that, culturally, we are on a very similar trajectory.

The German culture accommodated Hitler. What will we accommodate?

If you push human beings to the edge, if you have an extreme situation, almost anything can be justified. Remember my adage coming out of the White House: Human beings have an infinite capacity for self-rationalization.

I took communion this week. I always go into it in as genuinely a repentant state as I can be in. I know I should never be judgmental on life issues, because if it were not for my conversion and my belief that the Bible is God speaking, I would be a utilitarian. I'm a smart, well-educated person; I know that the best way to divide resources among people in a period of scarcity is to do the greatest good for the greatest number. It's eminently logical. But, of course, we Christians stand against the logic of the world.

# Brave New World

I would like to take you back in time and describe to you a laboratory in a gray building in London. In that laboratory there is a conveyer belt, and on that conveyer belt are little glass jars, and in those glass jars are fertilized ova, and they are clattering back and forth on the conveyer belt as they go from one side of the room to the other.

Those fertilized ova will break into ninety-six separate buds, and each one of those buds will mature into an embryo. Each one of those embryos will mature into a human being. Interestingly enough, the people who are conducting this experiment have figured out how to preprogram genetically what each person created in that test tube will be. Some will be laborers; some will be political leaders; some will be business leaders. They are all predestined.

I am talking about a scene from Aldous Huxley's 1931 novel *Brave New World*. This was maybe the most prophetic writing of the twentieth century—probably more prophetic than George Orwell's *1984*. If you remember the story of *Brave New World*, it is fascinating because of the parallels one can draw to what is happening in the biotech revolution today. The whole story of *Brave New World* is one of creating the ultimate utopian vision of the perfect society. Everybody would be given a pill, a narcotic, which will allow you to be lulled off into pleasure. If you felt any momentary depression, you just popped another pill into your mouth. Free sex was encouraged. Entertainment was the goal of the state—to entertain and amuse.

That is why Neil Postman, the great TV critic and professor at New York University, wrote that marvelous book some years ago, *Amusing Ourselves to Death*. In the introduction to his book, he used the *Brave New Word* parallel because what Huxley saw, Orwell didn't see. Orwell saw that there would be tyranny, but from totalitarian powers that would hold us in their grip. Huxley saw something different. Aldous Huxley said there would be tyranny all right, but it would be a tyranny in which you put all the people asleep. And then you amuse them constantly, keep them entertained, give them all the sex they want, and give them the drugs they want; and then you control them.

Those who give the entertainment and pleasure are the controllers of the society. Everybody is preprogrammed with a particular job because they are genetically determined. *Brave New World* is a great novel, by the way, if you haven't read it. It is marvelous entertainment. The great drama, the great plot, is based on a savage from New Mexico who still remembers his birth parents; he was not created in a test tube. He becomes subversive because he has a familial attachment. Therefore, he has to be exterminated, otherwise the whole experiment, which depends on dissolving the family, doesn't work. So the plot of *Brave New World* is how to get rid of this one person who is subversive, who still remembers what it is to have a mother and father.

You can certainly find parallels to some problems in today's society when you realize that all of the campaigns of the great utopian thinkers of our day were simply examples of what Huxley was prophesying. To control society, you've got to break down those structures which involve a person's fundamental loyalties, such as the family.

And that is what is behind the gay rights agenda. Many gays I have talked to don't really want to get married. They would much prefer the freedom they have of going from one relationship to another. But behind the entire agenda is an effort to weaken the family, because so long as the family becomes the primary source of loyalty to the individual, then the government, the powers-that-be, the cultural elite, or the media elite do not have ultimate control over how we live our lives.

That is really the heart of the book I wrote called *How Now Shall We Live?* I was trying to show that only a biblical understanding of reality, lived out in all of life, enables us to live together peacefully and in harmony and in concord with the way God created us. Otherwise it is a rebellion—the whole idea of personal autonomy.

Think about it! We have made autonomy the *summum bonum*, the ultimate good in American life. It rose out of the sixties. Personal autonomy is the perfect anti-God state. If you say, "I want to be autonomous," it might be one thing to be autonomous from political interference in your life, but autonomy in its definition is a rejection of God. Autonomy is the opposite state of dependence on the Creator.

We have seen every effort in the Supreme Court beginning with *Roe v. Wade* and through all its successive decisions to create this ultimate state of personal autonomy. But the way in which you really create it, the ultimate rebellion of shaking your fist at the Creator, is by saying; "I am not going to accept the fact that I have been created by God. I am going to create my own human race." And that is what Huxley saw.

# Ethical Science

Christians should never be antiscience or anti-progress. I can't be, because the more science discovers about DNA, the more it reflects, in my opinion, the truth that we are the products of an intelligent design.

Mathematics doesn't come about as a result of a chance occlusion of atoms in primordial soup; it can't be. The more we learn, the better our apologetic defense of Christian truth is. I am all for it.

What Huxley saw and what C. S. Lewis also saw, though coming from totally different perspectives, is that you can never separate science from moral truth. The only thing the Christian is saying is, "We welcome the biotech movement because it may well bring about great advances in human progress, and it is going to bring about a better understanding of the composition of the human body in such a way that it confirms what we believe about the intelligent design of human beings. But we want bioethics to have equal stature with biotechnology. We need to be able to look at what is right and wrong in our behavior and in our science."

We have been dominated in Western culture by what I call the "technological imperative." If something can be done, it will be done. And if you can invent something, you are going to invent it. The only question is who is asking whether we should do it!

Ethics deals with the "ought" factor; this is what we *ought* to do. Science deals with the *is* factor; this is what *is*. This is what can be done versus what ought to be done. The Christian brings a particular dimension to this debate, which is terribly important. We contribute the argument of what ought to be done, not what can be done. We may listen to science as it says what can be done, but then we must temper it always to the moral truth of what ought to be done.

# 3

# CHRISTIANS and PUBLIC LIFE

# The Roots of Liberty

**We Christians look at liberty the wrong way. We** believe we have to fight for the First Amendment because the First Amendment gives us liberty. No, it doesn't. Human freedom is rooted in the belief that this is the nature of God Himself, the One who created us. Remember, we are created in His image. Since God is free, we're free. It's our natural condition.

So the First Amendment doesn't give us any rights. The First Amendment *protects* rights that are already God given. And of course they can't be denied.

This presents a radical notion for a lot of Christians. Many Christians believe that we're to be concerned only with the religious liberty of other Christians—that we should fight against persecution and in favor of laws which protect fellow believers. But if we believe all human beings are made in the image of God, we must care about the religious liberties of everyone.

The Declaration of Independence got this right; we evangelicals more often than not get it wrong. We look at liberty from a very parochial perspective. The good news is that when we protect the rights of Christians, we are also protecting the rights of Muslims, Buddhists, Hindus, and atheists.

The nature of liberty is inherent in the character of God, and can never be reduced in any way. This is why civil disobedience isn't merely justified; it is mandated. If someone tries to deny us a liberty granted by God, or a human freedom which is part of God's nature, which we bear, we have to repudiate that.

When I was working with the folks at Evangelicals and Catholics Together, we thought we should talk less about religious liberty because it sounded as if we were talking about something we were liberated *from*. It sounded like something the state gives us, whereas in fact what we're talking about is the right to religious freedom because it is part of the very nature of God.

So when we argue about religious liberty, we're not arguing

that the state has given us some particular right. We are arguing that every human being is created in the image of God, as our founders emphasized in the Declaration of Independence, and therefore, has a free will, and liberty as an inalienable right.

# Jerry Falwell

*Few people brought Christians back into public life the way Jerry Falwell did. When Falwell died in 2007, Chuck dictated a memo recalling his relationship with him.*

Jerry Falwell was the victim of caricaturizing by the press. They loved the floppy jowls and the kind of overstuffed Southern preacher appearance. Then, of course, Jerry gave them some openings from time to time by saying some pretty flamboyant things.

But Jerry Falwell, along with Carl Henry and Billy Graham, deserves credit for bringing the fundamentalist Christian evangelical movement, which was cloistered during the first half of the twentieth century, into the mainstream of American culture. He also—though he didn't realize it—helped to do what Abraham Kuyper did in Holland: give Christians a way to get involved in the political arena and to engage it. I didn't like Jerry's strategy; I didn't like the Moral Majority. I thought it was too political. But God bless him, because he at least got the door open and mobilized the Christian church to stand against the encroachments on traditional values that were so aggressive in the wake of *Roe v. Wade* and in the hangover from the sixties.

On a purely personal note, I really liked Jerry. I listened to his advice very carefully when we picked a key employee for Prison Fellowship. I really trusted his judgment.

If you look at the great university he built, it is a phenomenal testimony to the son of a drunkard who grew up on the wrong side of the tracks to become one of the truly significant figures in American life.

Christians should be especially grateful to Jerry Falwell. His legacy will be far bigger than he was in life.

# A Matter of Conscience

*Whether the issue is charities, companies, and Christian colleges being forced to pay for "health care" that violates the consciences of those who run them, or Christian bakers being ordered to bake "wedding" cakes for homosexual couples or face high fines, Chuck warned of the wretched consequences to society if Christian organizations — in order to obey the God they serve — are forced to commit institutional suicide.*

On the subject of religious freedom and being forced to hire people who don't share our faith or don't agree to abide by our moral convictions—this issue is going to have a huge impact on the general public, because most AIDS shelters in America are maintained by Catholic Charities, and most homeless shelters by the Salvation Army. So they're really playing with fire here, because if you start closing those down (or if they close themselves down rather than violate the teachings of their faith), you're eliminating absolutely vital public services. There's got to be an exception on the hiring question.

But it's also going to raise a really serious question about whether we're willing to stand up for our faith, because the Salvation Army, once before in New York City, was ordered to comply with the city's hiring laws. Instead, it simply stopped taking $50 million from the city.

And that's what Christian organizations are going to have to do again. This is a time when, even as our funds are being restricted, we cannot give in on that demand. We cannot give our freedom away in the process. So this is really going to be a tough issue of conscience for us, as well as a huge political issue for the country.

I don't think people understand this is coming. But now that the eroding of religious liberties has started, they could be unraveled very quickly.

# The Law Beyond the Law

*In 1963, a Yale professor named Stanley Milgram devised a test to find out how willing people were to inflict what they were told were painful electric shocks on another person if an authority figure told them to. Some 80 percent were willing to do so.*

I just read an article in the *New York Times* titled, "Four Decades After Milgram, We're Still Willing to Inflict Pain." The reporter wrote, "It appears that ordinary Americans are about as willing to blindly follow orders to inflict pain on an innocent stranger as they were four decades ago."[1]

The results of the two experiments are a huge cautionary tale of how people respond to authority. The people who took part in the experiments followed orders apparently with their conscience never kicking in, telling them there was something wrong. It's one of the reasons our prisons are such brutal places. Those who run prisons have total authority over inmates, and they often brutalize them.

One of my first reactions reading this article is that nothing changes about human nature. We really do blindly follow authority. Very few people challenge it. It's not in our nature, despite the various social movements of the last thirty or forty years inviting us to challenge authority.

This is the reason why, when there's social chaos, people will choose order over liberty. It's the reason why, if you give a prison guard or a government clerk a little power, they become abusive.

My second reaction is that nothing could possibly have changed to affect the results of this experiment because the only barrier preventing people from inflicting pain is conscience. And conscience is often thought to be that little moral compass, something we feel inside of us, whether we feel something is right or wrong.

Which is nonsense. The word *conscience* comes from *conscienta*, which means "with knowledge." So your internal moral bearings have to be programmed. Romans 2:15 tells us the law is written on the heart. But our hearts have to be formed. And with the breakdown of the family and moral decay in American life, I'm not surprised in the slightest by the results of the experiments.

The experiments also raise the stickiest of ethical questions. When do you obey a lawful authority and when do you refuse to obey? That raises the whole question of civil disobedience. For the Christian, if you are being asked to obey a law that is contrary to the law of God, you follow the law of God. But with situations as with the Milgram experiment, you're being told to do something you know is wrong and yet you do it because you've been ordered to do it. This happened to me a few times in the White House. When a legitimate authority tells you to do something, how do you apply ethics in a case like this?

The answer is simple, really. You have to look for the law beyond the law, and be willing to courageously assert it. The best example I can think of is Martin Luther King Jr. writing his "Letter from a Birmingham Jail."[2]

But the fact is that people today have no concept of a law beyond the law. It isn't even on the radar screen. If there is no truth, as we are so often told these days, how could there be? In a morally relativistic era, there's nothing that kicks in and tells us something is wrong.

The final thing that strikes me about this is that the ultimate fear I think all of us have is that there will be a widespread moral and economic breakdown that will lead to chaos. And American citizens, given a choice between order and chaos, will always choose order—even if it shuts down some of our freedoms. One can see that happening in America.

# Consequences of the Fall

*During his long life, Chuck had witnessed a world war and seen great chaos break out in many countries. These experiences, added to his understanding of human nature and his time in the White House, made him fear what might happen in the United States if the financial crisis got bad enough. He warns of what happened in the past, in other countries, when this happened. His advice in August 2011 on how to respond to the economic crisis is applicable to crises we may face in the future.*

During a question-and-answer period following a meeting I recently participated in, I was asked whether the United States could survive the present crisis. It's a fair question and a relevant one.

We, as Christians, need to remember that the primary job of government, biblically, is to preserve order and do justice. Chaos is the enemy of the biblical understanding of government. That is why Romans 13 is so insistent upon obedience to the law and to governing authorities, because their authority comes from God.[3]

This understanding of government is incredibly important in a free society. Free societies exist only with the consent of the governed. If governing officials don't have the consent of the governed, they have to resort to force and authority. If they do have the consent of the governed, freedom can be preserved.

But the governed only give their consent when they have confidence in those who are governing them. If that confidence fails, then the whole experiment we have enjoyed in America—ordered liberty—fails as well.

What do we make of the current situation? Financial markets around the world are in a state of absolute chaos. Uncertainty reigns. I've never known a time when the American people seemed so frightened and frustrated. The polls show that 80 percent of the American people believe the country is on the wrong track. This is not sustainable.

Remember what happened in the thirties with the Germans. They were in a sustained crisis of confidence and the economy was failing. Germans were buying their groceries with wheelbarrows full of marks to purchase them; their money had become worthless. Chaos broke out in the streets, much of it prompted by Hitler, who then stepped forward and said he would restore order. And under those circumstances the people greeted him as a conquering hero. They welcomed surrendering their liberty for order.

That's the human condition. That's the consequence of the fall. God forbid it would ever happen in our free society.

So what is the number one priority to preserve order and justice in society today? Bring our leaders together with an absolute ironclad commitment to cut $6 trillion off our deficit. A combination of tax reform and judicious cuts would do it. We would be restored as the prime currency in the world. America would once again be the beacon of confidence and hope for the rest of the world.

And those of us in the church need to be very careful. Don't fan the fears of collapse; just instruct Christians how to be biblically faithful every day of the week.

That was my answer to the question "Can America survive?" Of course it can, particularly if we, the people of God, act with confidence in God's ultimate sovereignty and do our job day in and day out.

# Combating Atheist Garbage

I just read an article by Harvey Mansfield,[4] who is one of the lonely conservatives on Harvard's faculty. I don't know anything about his religious persuasion, but this was an incredibly well-argued piece in response to all the atheist garbage. Two points he made are extremely important. The first had to do with all the name-calling atheists engage in against Christians, Christopher Hitchens in particular. A lot of it is aimed at "fanatics" like Jerry Falwell and Pat Robertson. The religious right has been compared to the Taliban and called "theocrats"—extremely pejorative terms designed to inflame anger against us.

But who's really the fanatic here? Look at the way Mansfield makes this argument; it's lovely. Falwell, for all of his bluster, did a lot of things to help the poor. He welcomed gays to his church. Christians are basically loving. Atheists have no real basis for love, other than fleeting emotions. If, in this debate over how we live and what we believe, and what organizes our lives together, we are called fanatics by people who are themselves this fanatical, it just becomes a name-calling contest. Nobody is going to make any intelligent decisions based on this kind of talk. But the hypocrisy of it is really appalling. I'll bet these atheists don't even see that they are engaged in much more inflammatory rhetoric than anything any Christian has ever said.

They also mischaracterize God as an angry God, which He is not. He has every right to be angry at sin, but He's also dealt with it in the most loving way possible: by sending His own Son as an offering.

Mansfield also noted that the Epicurean atheism of the ancient world was very different from ours. It was looking for tyranny, as Mansfield put it, behind the mask of religion. But it was content to simply point out the power of injustice, not to eradicate religion.

This brings us to the second point: the justice question. Mansfield put this beautifully. I have always argued, as I did in *The Good Life* and again in *The Faith*, that people have an innate knowledge that there is right and wrong, which drives a compelling desire to see justice done. Even atheists shake their fist at people who cut them off in traffic, saying, "Someday you'll get yours." Even atheists take great pleasure seeing evil punished, even though they say there's no such thing as evil. It's built into us; this is part of the way we're made. This is part of the *imago Dei* in us.

In the Christian perspective, the very character of God is justice. He is so concerned with justice that He takes our sin seriously. But He is also loving, so He provides a way for us to be forgiven and restored. Nonetheless, the demands of justice sent Christ to the cross.

We also understand biblical justice, as I've written *ad nauseam*, in a totally different way than human justice. Human justice is balancing scales, which both atheists and Christians would agree is right. But biblical justice goes way beyond it; it goes to *shalom*, to producing those conditions in which there is genuine harmony and concord and human flourishing.

The atheist, as Mansfield quite rightly pointed out, has no basis for this. So if there is nothing that requires people to do good or evil, or even to recognize them (and Richard Dawkins says there is no such thing as good or evil), then on what basis can you organize a system of justice? You can't. You simply have to put someone in power and hope they're going to be just. You appoint people to a court and hope they'll be just, but there's no objective standard by which justice can be measured. And I think Mansfield is brilliant in pointing out that Germany, the country of Kant, who produced the categorical imperative, which is the best ethical formulation a secularist could offer (it's really the Golden Rule dressed up a bit), ended up with atheistic totalitarianism in the twentieth century.

Justice can only be achieved if there is an overarching standard of right and wrong, of truth, by which we can measure human behavior—reward what is good, punish what is wrong. It is on this point that the whole atheistic case collapses.

In my opinion, this is why they're so angry; it's why they keep calling us names. They know full well that they can't achieve a system of justice, that their only way of advancing their agenda is through power. I think this is really the crux of it.

# A Cacophony of Self-Interest

Archbishop Donald Wuerl of Washington, DC, and I spent some time talking recently at a dinner about the fact that politicians have an express duty to seek the common good. I think he was talking in the Catholic tradition, because I don't know where else there would be an express duty. Or maybe he was just using the term loosely. But it struck me as a very poignant term. We talked about it in the Manhattan Declaration [a 2009 political manifesto now signed by more than half a million people] quite deliberately—that our job [as Christians] is to seek the common good and do justice.

The whole problem in American public life today is that the concept of the common good has been lost, destroyed by our blurring distinctions between good and evil. If there is no evil, then there's no good; just as it's true that if there is no good, called law, then there could be no transgression. I was just reading Romans 4:15 in my devotional: "Where there is no law, there is no transgression." This is Augustine's point, that the opposite of the good is the non-good.

But in the age of relativism, we can't make those judgments. So we can no longer call wrong wrong, or good good. So the whole notion of politicians working for the common good suffers. Who is to say what the common good is? Is it everybody's subjective opinions? That's just a cacophony of self-interest. It can't be.

So who defines the common good? It's been the great tradition. It's the virtues and values that we seek to inculcate in society; it's the things we talk about that are good in our founding documents and the things that are bad. But this, in a politically correct relativistic culture, requires all kinds of judgments to be made.

I think this is only one of the reasons why politicians today no longer think in terms of the common good. Probably a more obvious reason is that politics has become such an expensive business. Even running for the state senate in Virginia costs over $100,000. So you're ultimately going to be beholden to special interests unless you get a remarkably broad base of donors, which is impossible today. Obama said he did it, but he did not. He had a lot of fat cats on Wall Street and Hollywood who raised buckets of money for him, especially George Soros. Unfortunately this has really corrupted the political process.

We need to resurrect the now-forgotten, virtually neglected notion of the common good being the goal of someone in public office. And with all the special interest scandals, with all the self-dealing, the common good has been trampled into the ground. But this is a useful concept to resurrect and talk about.

# Praying for the Church

In my devotions over the last two or three weeks, I started my prayer time by concentrating on the church, and praying that the Lord would energize us, wake us up, cause us to repent and turn from our own false idols, and love God and advance His kingdom. Then I prayed for leaders of the church and I prayed for my family, and the country, because my heart ached, seeing what was happening, particularly in the credit crisis at the time and the wrong way we were going about solving it.

It hit me like a ten-ton truck that the priority of my prayer was absolutely right. You can't pray for your nation to be revived, to be saved, to have God's mercy, to make wise decisions and get out of the mess we were in with the sub-prime crisis unless you first prayed for the church, because the country couldn't get out of the hole it was in. When you're in a hole, you're supposed to stop digging. We were continuing to dig. And we got in the hole by getting too much credit. So now we wanted to get out of the hole by getting more credit?

This crisis of character was caused when we traded a Christian worldview of work and of the economy for a false worldview of consumerism. It's a false worldview that leads to the worst kind of idolatries. But it will also lead to our self-destruction.

I want to put this in the bluntest terms I can: This nation cannot be saved unless the church is saved first. Renewing the church is the key to saving America. I don't know whether America still has a special place in God's sovereign plans for the world; I could argue that many times over the 230-odd years we've been a nation we have had that special place, and most of our founders saw this. This is what we call American exceptionalism, the idea that we have a worldwide role to play.

No other nation is going after the problem of AIDS in Africa like we are. That's an example of American exceptionalism. That's an example of America having a manifest destiny, if you will, to do good in the world. And by and large, that's our history.

But we will be unable to continue that if we are bankrupt. And the fact is, we are nearly bankrupt because of the overindulgence in credit and the self-indulgence of our people. So, in come all the politicians who say, okay, let's throw some more money here; let's pump funds in and get people spending again, which is what got us into trouble in the first place. It's not going to solve the problem. We need to reorganize, just like anyone does in bankruptcy.

The critical point is that America cannot be saved if the church is not first revived. My prayer priorities were correct. These should be the priorities of other Christians too. If we don't learn how to do the very best of things and teach worldview to our neighbors and use this calamity (which the credit crisis was for so many millions of people) as a teaching opportunity, then we're simply not going to be doing the job of the church. And if the church doesn't do its job, I don't see another generation coming for America.

# Bring on the Bulldozers

The purpose of government is to preserve order and do justice. It is for the common good. It is certainly not what government can do for you.

In 1963, President John F. Kennedy offered a memorable challenge in his inaugural address: "Ask not what your country can do for you; ask what you can do for your country."

Today, by contrast, politicians pander to us. Hillary Clinton reversed Kennedy's challenge during the 2008 primary elections; she said not to think about what this election would mean for the country; instead, she said, think about what it would mean for you. Our tax cuts would give you more money to spend. We're going to have more special dispensations for this or that. This would help you and your family.

This is nonsense. Whoever is elected president is going to face huge crises. We have demands on us internationally; we have Medicare being subsidized by the general budget; we have both candidates promising some universal health coverage. And the country is broke.

The only way this country is going to survive is if somebody drives into Washington on bulldozers and starts dismantling this corrupt system where K Street lobbyists pay their money, buy their congressmen, and their congressmen turn around and vote for what the lobbyists want. And never in this process does anyone even stop to think what's good for the country as a whole.

But here's the thing to remember: it's never been any different. Recently in my devotions I was reading Hosea, which speaks about how Israel had prostituted itself, worshiping the surrounding nations' idols, and becoming as vile as the things they loved. And so the Lord says, in 10:3, "Then they will say, 'We have no king, because we did not revere the LORD.'" This is certainly what the United States has done.

But even if we had a king, the verse goes on, "what could he do for us?" And then the Lord gives us the answers. The leaders, or the kings, "make many promises, take false oaths and make agreements; therefore lawsuits spring up like poisonous weeds in a plowed field."

I've never read anything that so accurately describes the situation in America today. The whole agenda of government is to pander to one special interest group or another, to build a consensus. But it's all based on personal interest. Everyone does what is right in his own eyes.

We have gotten away from the understanding of what our founders called nature and nature's God, the idea that there is a transcendent authority and some sense of responsibility that we have for each other and for the common good. There's no basis to talk about the common good. So what we have instead is a collection of special, personal interests, and the country is falling apart before our eyes. We are seeing take place today what took place in Hosea's Israel.

I'm not unaware that as I say this people will think of me as a maniac and a fool. That's exactly what God says happened to the prophets of that day. In Hosea 9:7, He describes the sins being so great, the hostilities so great, that the prophet is considered a fool, the inspired man a maniac.

Well, you can write me off as a fool and a maniac if you wish. Will anybody wake up? The book of Hosea has made a lot of things clear to me, including the fact that nations are destroyed, and people are destroyed, because they reject knowledge. That is, they ignore the laws of God. As is written in Hosea 4:6, "My people are destroyed from lack of knowledge."

# 4

# CHURCH
## and CULTURE

# A Stern Monitor

*When Chuck was engaging in his teaching ministries —*
*especially* BreakPoint *— he never took his eyes off the next generation.*
*He worried constantly about the messages the culture was sending*
*them — including his five grandchildren — and regularly advised parents*
*and churches on how to counteract its harmful messages.*

*Many, many* BreakPoint *commentaries ended with something along*
*the lines of "Tell your neighbors around the backyard barbeque, tell your*
*Bible study group, tell your children and grandchildren about this ..."*
*It's still excellent advice.*

So often these days we hear the phrase, *Let your conscience be*
*your guide.* And maybe some of you parents have told that to your
kids. If you have, it's the worst advice you can possibly give them.

In this relativistic era, we interpret conscience to be a matter of
our feelings, how we feel about certain things. But anybody who
has done any counseling at a church or anywhere else knows that
you will have people come to you, describe some horrible transgression, and then say, "Well, I really felt I was doing the right thing."

I learned from my White House days that the human capacity
for self-justification and self-rationalization is infinite. We really
know how to make ourselves feel good about doing bad.

So what is conscience? How do we know it's going to be a reliable guide for us?

The famous British cleric Cardinal John Henry Newman called
conscience "a stern monitor." This means our conscience is not,
as philosopher Russell Hittinger put it, "the writer of permission slips." Conscience is that part of our psyche that holds in
focus what is objectively good and what is objectively bad, and it
restrains the human passions from doing what is bad, and guides
it to do what is right.

Notice he uses the word *objective.* The etymology of *conscience*
is in the Latin—*conscienta*, which means "with knowledge."

So what we do in raising children, or in building our own character, is to steep ourselves in what the moral law is. As Christians, we steep ourselves in biblical teaching for the purpose of informing our conscience.

This is not an overnight process; this is something that is done on a long-term basis. You've got to start with kids when they're four and five years old, and work with them until they're in their teens, and then keep reminding them. Adults must reflect on various moral issues, and read and study and pray so that we *know* what is right, and then develop the will to do it.

Developing the will to do what our conscience tells us is, of course, another matter. That is, shaping our character so that the distorted human will, perverted as it is away from good and toward evil, is bent back toward good. That's what we mean by developing character, developing the will to do what is right. But the conscience comes first. You have to know what it is.

Let your conscience be your guide? Okay—but only if it is informed by what is true.

# Liberty and Chaos

I read an article in the *Wall Street Journal* titled, "As If Things Weren't Bad Enough, Russian Professor Predicts End of U.S."[1] It really was frightening. This Russian academic, who works at a think tank, had been predicting for years that America would break up, the result, he said, of a moral and economic collapse.

This is really cause for some concern, because when societies decay they usually implode, just like the Russian empire did. They implode because they lose the moral authority to govern, and people choose order over liberty to avert chaos. It happened to the Germans in 1932. That's how Hitler came to power. And perfectly decent German citizens cheered him by the millions, even as he went after the Jews, because he was going to lead them out of the chaos they were living in, hyperinflation produced, just like we're going to face, I think.

The interesting thing about this prediction by a Russian professor about the end of the United States is that it sounded so implausible, improbable, off the wall. But I remember in the mid-eighties when Reagan said something about bringing down the Soviet empire, everybody mocked him. No one in our intelligence apparatus—and I've had friends in it over the years who tell me a lot of what goes on—ever once really believed that the Soviet empire would collapse.

I talked to government officials who told me that Kissinger wouldn't believe it when the first indications of the collapse were taking place. There were articles printed, even in the late eighties, that the great threat would be Russia emerging as an ever-stronger superpower, overpowering us with their missiles. People did not see the Soviet Union's demise coming.

When I was in the Soviet Union, I asked whether people inside saw it coming. I was there in 1991, I think, maybe 1990. And the answer was "no." Nobody had any idea that this was going to happen. It happened because they spent themselves into bankruptcy. Gorbachev saw it coming and tried to put the brakes on and convert to a less totalitarian form of government, or at least preserve as much as he could of the prior model, and of course that collapsed, people filled the streets in Moscow, and for a while it looked like Russia would become a democracy. But instead it collapsed on a course not unlike the one we're on—funding guns and butter.

So when you begin to ask yourself the question of how important are the moral structures of society, how important are they to an economy, and what kind of a protection are they against tyranny, you realize how vulnerable we have become by jettisoning Judeo-Christian traditions and values. We have taught people there is no truth and there's nothing they need to worry about except to get whatever they can get and live for today and forget about tomorrow. This is the logical conclusion if we continue the course we're on. I don't mean to be an alarmist, but I really believe this. I really believe if we don't have a renewal we will lose Western civilization.

From the standpoint of the kingdom of God, maybe that doesn't matter. Maybe the kingdom will move to China and we'll see a renewal of Christianity and the building of a Christian culture there. It's very possible. But we are the exhausted volcano in the West that William Gladstone talked about. We're running out of steam, and it's because of our lack of commitment to truth. It's what Pope John Paul II has been warning about for a decade.

And we're there.

Let's not cause people to run for their bomb shelters, but let's at least make them aware of the stakes that are involved here as we face the moral decline of Western civilization.

# The Danger of Sloth

I read a superb piece by Meghan Cox Gurdon in the *Wall Street Journal*.[2] She was really onto something. Moral neutrality is not neutral, certainly not in a fallen world. And this is the whole problem with our politically correct culture. It allows us to pander to our worst instincts.

I love the way Gurdon ties this piece to the original Emily Post, back in the 1920s. There was a time when Emily Post set the standards for social behavior. That's because there *were* standards for social behavior. Today there are none, so people simply do whatever they please.

What gave those standards force was the fact that there was cultural acceptance and cultural pressure. In other words, you wouldn't do certain things because they weren't the kind of practices that people would accept. There were taboos and limits on what was considered appropriate under certain circumstances. People were concerned with what has now become a very quaint term: *decorum* — the proper behavior, the proper attitude, the proper clothing.

These are the things, whether we like it or not, which civilize society. I wrote some years ago that Americans were dressing down and engaging in public slothfulness, which basically shows a lack of self-regard and self-respect. And when you lose respect for yourself, you lose respect for others. There really is a case to be made for manners. When William Wilberforce was talking about the reformation of manners, he was talking about the values and the attitudes and the way we live. That's the broader sense of manners.

There is no way you can deal with moral issues without moral instruction. We need to teach our children that moral neutrality is permissiveness. It is abandoning the sense that there is a moral standard.

Second, a civil society demands civility, decorum, appropriate behavior and dress—taboos enforced by cultural pressures. If you don't have that, you're going to have chaos.

Today's hook-up culture is a direct consequence of the loss of this essential virtue. There's a reason why slothfulness is one of the seven deadly sins.

# How Not to Witness

G. K. Chesterton was once invited to a meeting of the leading intellectuals in England. They were all asked to answer the same question: If they were shipwrecked on a deserted island, what one book would they want to have with them?

Chesterton was a prominent Christian, and everybody knew that he would want to have the Bible with him. But when his turn came to speak, Chesterton's answer was, "Why, *A Practical Guide to Shipbuilding*, of course."

The point is that oftentimes we need to understand things that are not covered in the Bible. And we need to understand things that help us apply biblical teachings. This is why I teach biblical worldview. We have to understand how the Bible intersects with all of life.

A man once told Oswald Chambers that he read only the Bible. Chambers replied, "My strong advice to you is to soak, soak, soak in philosophy and psychology until you know more of these subjects than you ever need consciously to know. When people refer to a man as a man of one book, meaning the Bible, he is generally found to be a man of multitudinous books, which simply isolates the one book in its proper grandeur."[3]

There's a reason for this. When we go into public discussions, particularly with secular neighbors, we need to understand how to present the biblical case. For example, I've given talks about how I've gone into state legislatures all across America and said we must have restitution instead of imprisonment and in a lot of cases pay back the victims and restore the offender to society. Whenever I give that talk, people come up to me afterward and say, "That restitution is a great idea. Where did it come from?"

Then I tell them it is exactly what Moses taught in the Old Testament and Jesus taught in the New Testament. It comes right from the Bible. And that becomes a good opportunity for witness.

We recently finished filming at Princeton an ethics series called "Doing the Right Thing."[4] Brit Hume was the moderator; Robert George of Princeton and I were the cohosts. Every principle that we taught was biblically based. But in very few instances did we use the Bible as authority. The reason is, we wanted our ethics course taught in secular colleges and business schools. You have to preach in language accessible to the frame of reference your listener has.

It's a sad fact in our post-Christian culture, but to start a conversation today by saying "the Bible says" will often cause the listener to stop listening or turn off what you say. I wish that weren't the case, but it is. So what you do is make arguments based on what the Reformers called common grace, or what historically has been called natural law. And try to make them accessible to your listener.

Bear in mind this is what Paul did when he first went to Athens, Greece, the center of sophistication and learning in the world. Remember that Acts 17 says that he reasoned with the Jews in the marketplace in Thessalonica. In other words, he made well-reasoned arguments. And then in his great sermon at Mars Hill, he quoted Greek poets; he referred to Greek artifacts. He thoroughly engaged their culture. He had learned what they believed, and then used their belief to lead them directly into the gospel, and then of course the resurrection. This is a model for us.

This is why it is so important for us to study biblical worldview, comparing how the Bible works out in life versus how other systems of thought do. The biblical view will give you the rational answer. When you neglect biblical truths, then life becomes irrational.

# The Ties That Loosen

*To say that Chuck was a huge C. S. Lewis fan would be a massive understatement. Outside of biblical authors, I wouldn't doubt that Chuck quoted the Oxford don more than any other source. Lewis had much to say about the right way to live our lives, and Christians who believe they can get by on reading the Bible alone are missing out on great wisdom.*

Rereading C. S. Lewis recently has reminded me of how enormous the cultural shift has been from the forties and fifties until today. In the long span of history, that's a pretty short period of time. And yet the world has changed dramatically.

Now, people my age always say things have changed, and they always seem to think change is bad, but I'm not saying that. I think we've experienced an unusual shift, similar to a tectonic shift in the plates of the earth. For instance, we've gone from a community-centered culture in the West to being so self-absorbed that we can best be described as narcissistic. Christopher Lasch's book on the culture of narcissism was dead-on, and that was nearly forty years ago. How much worse this problem is today.

Here's my question as I think about that shift. Why is it that, all of a sudden, the United States, which has the safest currency in the world and the strongest economy in the world, is absolutely shaking? We don't have long before debt payment will reach a percentage of the GNP that makes it impossible for us to maintain our ratings with Moody and Standard and Poor's. That's not far off. And any slight increase in interest rates, and it's "Katy bar the door" because we can't pay the debt. But it's not just us; the same thing has been happening in Spain, Italy, Portugal, and of course in Greece. And what we're seeing, when benefits are cut, are riots in the street—everywhere from England and Greece to Madison, Wisconsin.

Is this debt crisis just the 2008 bubble bursting, or is it something deeper? Is it possible that what is happening to free societies in the West is that we are so focused on ourselves, so determined to get "what we're entitled to," so absorbed with our own desires and interests that we can't see the greater good of the community?

Alexis de Tocqueville believed that the great cardinal virtue that dominated America was the idea of civic responsibility and civic duty. Our founders steeped us in that tradition. That's basically gone; it has disappeared, and not just here: It has disappeared in Europe as well. In the more rural cultures in Europe—Italy, Germany, England, and Ireland—communities banded together. They all worked together and then met in the pub at night.

I haven't observed those cultures closely enough in the last ten years, but I suspect those ties that bind us together are loosening. It's the inevitable consequence of rampant individualism, what Robert Bellah calls "ontological individualism." But free societies simply cannot survive this way. If people aren't willing to take care of their own responsibilities, if they are not concerned with their neighborhood, their state, and their society, if it's all about them and nothing else, then we're going to have debt crises, because we're not going to have responsibility in how we spend money. We're going to depend on trying to get somebody else's money to do it for us.

I'm wondering if what we're seeing in the world is not a terrifying manifestation of what C. S. Lewis saw coming in *The Aboli-*

*tion of Man,* when people lost their respect for "the Tao," a shared set of traditional moral values, and began to look out only for themselves. Man's conquest of nature becomes nature's conquest of man. Lewis really nailed it. And when it got to that point, how did he say we would see people behaving? We'd see free societies running wild, unable to control themselves, their appetites, or their passions, and beginning to self-destruct.

Is it a stretch to say that's what is happening in the Western world? It's not happening in China or India; it's happening in the West, the very foundation of what we call Western civilization, which we've always considered the most humane and liberal society ever created.

One thing is certain: We have lost the capacity to restrain our baser passions and instincts. What remains of the free societies of the West? We're dealing with the consequences of false ideas being lived out, false worldviews having taken over the hearts and minds of people in the advanced societies of the world. Tragic to watch, isn't it?

The job of the church, of course, is to counter the false worldviews gripping our culture and to defend what is true, beautiful, and just. It almost seems like an impossible task, and it is, without God's intervention. But nonetheless, that's the job we've got to do.

# Dominion and the Environment

We need to debunk the idea that man is invading the pristine beauty and wilderness—that man is the problem, destroying the beauty of the earth.

I like the way the Acton Institute puts it: Man is not despoiling the environment; he is cultivating it. He is improving it and replacing it with a different kind of beauty—a beauty that is productive, which takes care of human needs. This is the real meaning of "take dominion" in Genesis 1.[5]

The earth did not just stay untouched and beautiful, but was converted, and was still beautiful, because from it came productivity that enhanced humankind.

The problem with the environmental movement today is that it is almost 100 percent antipeople. They see population control or even the elimination of people as the answer to environmental degradation.

The Christian, on the other hand, sees that he has a stewardship responsibility to people and the environment, and that the job of cultivating and tilling is to make the environment all the more productive and beneficial for the good of human beings, without, of course, despoiling it. We're talking about the beauty of human productivity and creativity, given the rich minerals and resources of the land and of the world in which we live and the cycles of nature.

Our job is to cultivate and till, to enhance life, God's supreme creation, which is the human being. But we must do it in a way that is productive of the earth's resources and not despoiling.

So humans are not the enemy. They're God's agents for making the fullest use of the resources God has given us, and sustaining and propagating human flourishing. And this is where we break with the "green" movement. The green movement puts the earth first. It is a superbly naturalistic view of reality, whereas we take a theistic view. We see the ultimate creative act of God in creating humans in His own image, which nature is not. Nor, of course, are animals.

This is where the two worldviews really collide.

# In His Hands

This is a time when people are really wringing their hands. I've never seen such anxiety over the threats of terrorism, the shaken economy, and possible job loss. All the polls show an amazing insecurity among Americans, with a majority of us thinking our country is on the wrong track.

This is where our Christian faith should kick in and give us a perspective with which we can view these events. We must not succumb to despair, even if the whole world is; despair is a sin because it denies the sovereignty of God.

Our job is not to figure out how all of these cosmic events are going to work out—what our relations will be with China, whether the unemployment rate will start down or not. Our job is simply to do what God has called us to do, one day at a time, and do it as well as we possibly can, leaving the outcome in His hands.

People have accused me of being an optimist when I talk this way. But it isn't a question of optimism. Optimism comes from the word *optics*, that is, how you see things. We're not talking about how you see things or perceive things; we're talking about how God will respond to events, and how He will use us as part of His response.

Philippians 4:8—one of my favorite passages of Scripture because it talks about keeping your mind on things that are good and strong and true—supports this idea.

# Chronicles of Wasted Time

In the late seventies I gave an interview in Ireland in which I said I feared nothing since becoming a Christian. Len LeSourd caught me on that, and challenged me afterward. It was a very sobering experience. I learned a good lesson. I would never say that again.[6]

The fear of God is not what we think it is, however. The fear of God doesn't mean you shake in your boots when you're listening to the sermon of Jonathan Edwards, although that is fear of God. Fear is reverence, and it means to hold Him in a lofty position, and not to treat Him in a profane or trivial way. This is the missing ingredient in the church today.

Years ago I visited Pompeii, where centuries ago, people were going about their daily lives in one of the most advanced cultures in the world, and suddenly the molten ash from Mount Vesuvius came and swept over them like Hurricane Katrina swept over

New Orleans. They were absolutely vaporized in place, although bodies could be made out in the ash. They were annihilated in a split second. But the whole culture was left in place and preserved by the hot molten ash.

It's really chilling because when I visited Pompeii I realized that we hang by a slender thread, just like Jonathan Edwards preached. We could be wiped out tomorrow. We could be paralyzed tomorrow by a dirty bomb going off in the city in which we live. We have no guarantee that the US won't have a crisis of confidence and collapse into chaos and anarchy. Without a moral code, that can happen to any society. It's held together in the most fragile way by a system of laws and interlocking systems, but if we have sudden chaos, as we saw in Katrina, the whole thing collapses before you.

When you get to my age, which is seventy-three, you begin to think about what really makes life matter. You come to the same conclusion Solomon did. I can really identify with Ecclesiastes. I think back on my life, and recall the title of Malcolm Muggeridge's autobiography, *Chronicles of Wasted Time*. So much is vanity of vanities. So much is striving against the wind. And yet you come to the conclusion Solomon came to: in the end, what really matters is fearing God and keeping His commandments.

Somehow I'd like to get a bracing dose of this understanding through the church.

# A House of Cards

Someone told me he saw a poll recently in which 80 percent of the American people had expressed loss of confidence in government. My first reaction was, well, this is what these jokers in high office have done; they've undermined the authority of government. And that happens in lots of instances. It has never happened with serious consequences in America, thank God, but it has around the world, most prominently in Latin America.

The reason there has been such total political instability in Latin America—with banana republics collapsing and constant changes of regimes and revolutionaries—is that the people have lost all trust in government. Remember when liberation theology failed in Latin America, everyone was startled. The proponents of liberation theology thought the people would buy it and love it because it would provide all the government largesse to them. And the people rejected it. The people had lost all confidence in government; they didn't trust it. So the minute you tied the gospel to government, people said, whoa, I don't want that; I don't trust them. Good object lesson there, as a matter of fact.

But if 80 percent or even 50 percent of the American people have lost confidence in their government, this is a shocking statistic.

The reason it's so shocking is that government reacts by exercising more authority and grabbing more power, simply because it can't afford to lose its grip on the people. And if people aren't confident in government and aren't willing to continue to support it and give it their allegiance, then the government is going to fall. But governments don't fall gently or readily. The Soviet Union did, that's right, and we could, that's true, but only after the government has taken every effort it can possibly take to tighten the reins of power. That's what happened in the Soviet Union. They tightened it so much that it finally burst apart. But China is continuing to do it today. And we would do it. We would do the Latin American route, and the ultimate consequence would be either a revolution or the establishment of a permanent tyranny. Tocqueville warned about all of it.

The point needs to be made that Congress has become a house of rogues, and the White House is not much better. The Secretary of the Treasury, Timothy Geithner, has been confirmed even though he hasn't paid his taxes. And the worst thing is, there really wasn't a lot of outrage about it. Earmarks are now so embedded in the congressional culture that I don't think they will ever be abandoned. You'd have to change the whole structure of Congress. The Democrats used them shamefully when they controlled

the Congress; the Republicans came in and advanced it even further—used them worse!

Then after Obama's election the Democrats were back in, having thrown out those Republican rogues, and they were doing it
again, even hanging earmarks onto the health care reform bill.
This is shameless.

All Americans have had to deal with the Department of Motor
Vehicles, which notified me once that my license was being sus-
pended because I didn't have insurance, which was not true. So I
went through a lot of red tape to try to get it back, and you cannot
talk to anybody who will help you; it's just impossible. Anybody
who has had to deal with the Social Security Administration or
Medicare will tell you that it's an absolute rat's nest. You can't get
anything done, even when you want to give money back to the
government, which I did once. Now we see the US Postal Service
falling apart; people don't think they can get a letter posted.

Just look at the things government does, and measure your
own satisfaction with them, and measure public attitudes generally, and you will see that people are dissatisfied with very good
reason, because the government has taken on so much and has
become such a leviathan and is so bureaucratically encrusted. The
government employees' unions have so much power, and the government has just piled program upon program and has become
unwieldy and ungovernable.

Only two things can happen. The government is not going
to reform itself. So you either have tyranny or revolution—
ultimately. But the process of tyranny will be what Tocqueville
predicted it would be—a slow, creeping growth of benign despotism. Like a deadly cancer it is now metastasizing, and we're
seeing that happen in our midst.

The only thing that could possibly avert it is a powerful
spiritual awakening in the country which would lead people to
realize that, from a biblical perspective, government has gone
far beyond its mandate and has to be reined in, and eventually will be reined in because there will be a revolution. But
that could be forestalled if there were an absolute earthquake

at an election where every incumbent was turned out, and only people promising term limits got elected.

The public would really have to take a "plague on both your houses" attitude. Or maybe some candidate will emerge who will promise to serve one term, shut down half the agencies—all the ones that are needless—and be backed by a Congress that decides public service is more important than private interest.

I've met a few congressmen who fit that category, but unfortunately, they are very few and far between. Look at the failure of Congressman Frank Wolf's very moderate, modest proposal for a commission to figure out all the needed cuts and demand an up-or-down vote.

Maybe we'll go bankrupt before all this happens, and then the whole thing will cave in. Otherwise, if confidence in government continues to decline, you've only got those two possible conclusions. Wake up!

# Fact versus Fiction

America's newspaper of record, the *New York Times*, has joined the growing chorus of news outlets demanding that candidates for public office who are Christian affirm their respect not only for the separation of church and state, but as the *Times* puts it, "for the separation of fact and fiction."

While I would hope that any candidate for office wanted to protect separation of church and state—this commitment, after all, was brought to our shores by Christians fleeing a state church in Europe and has been a staple of American Christianity—I would also hope that all candidates, not just Christians, are able to separate fact and fiction.

The *Times* salvo was fired by Bill Keller, retiring executive editor. As a fallen-away Catholic, Keller really should know better. The first task, it seems to me, would be to get one's facts straight. He listed Rick Perry, Michele Bachmann, and Rick Santorum as being affiliated with "fervid subsets of evangelical Christianity." Fact check number one: Rick Santorum is a devout Roman Catholic.

The thrust of Keller's concerns centered on whether candidates believe their faith should inform their behavior, and whether they have received divine instructions on how we should be governed.

How does anyone separate his deepest convictions about reality from how he believes we should live our lives and be governed in society? Mr. Keller, who apparently no longer believes in God, shouldn't separate that core conviction from how he thinks people should live any more than I should believe that the God who created us in His image and gave us human dignity has nothing to say about protecting that human dignity.

The founding fathers had no problem with this. "We hold these truths to be self-evident, that all men are created equal, and endowed by their Creator with certain inalienable rights."

I wonder if I would vote for a candidate who couldn't affirm that. That was the foundational document of this country. Isn't that a good thing?

Martin Luther King Jr., whose monument is being unveiled now in Washington, DC, insisted that a law of the government that was contrary to the law of God was no law at all. That was the basis of his civil disobedience. Thank God he understood that very plain teaching of St. Augustine and the Bible.

Mr. Keller seems all in a dither over Governor Perry's relationship with a historian who says that we ought to have a government "firmly rooted in biblical principles." It seems to me the founders were very clear about that. This was not a Christian nation; this was founded as an open and free democracy in which all citizens could live together, regardless of their faith. But the underlying moral consensus referred to repeatedly by the founders was the Judeo-Christian value system. That's been clear until recent times in our law and in our common understanding.

In fact, where would we be without it? What does a Christian really believe about government? We know from the Old Testament that it has two great purposes: preserving order and doing justice—certainly important contributions to the common good. And we know from the New Testament that we are to obey the law, that we are to be, as Augustine said, the best of citizens, because we do out of love for God what others do only because they're required to. That hardly sounds seditious. And yet this is the overwhelming teaching of the Christian church.

Sure, we have some flaky movements in Christianity. One that I've taken strong exception to is "reconstruction" or "dominionism." Keller really gets worked up over this, believing that Michele Bachmann, Rick Perry, and others have formed some unholy alliance with the dominionists.

What he fails to understand is that this is a tiny fringe movement within the evangelical church. Using the state to enforce the law on the part of the church was a serious mistake in earlier centuries, long since corrected. No respected Christian leader truly believes that the Bible should be the law of the land.

When dealing with religious belief systems, which are often very complex, we have to be very careful that we don't tar everybody with the same brush. Keller seems to want to tar us with the so-called dominionist movement. I personally don't know any adherents to it. But if a Christian were to say that all Muslims are in sympathy with the jihadists, he would be denounced as an extreme bigot—and rightly so.

Should faith inform our public actions? That's the real question that we come down to. Mario Cuomo, then governor of New York, valiantly tried in 1984 to say that he could be personally opposed to something—a profound moral issue in this case—but nonetheless publicly support it because it was the law of the land. Not so easily can most of us compartmentalize ourselves. The job of a Christian office holder who is asked to do something that violates his conscience is not to "impose" his views on the state—how would you ever do that in a democracy anyway?—it is to step down; or alternatively, to work hard to change the public attitude.

Of course our core values inform what we do—and should!

I think we all need to cool down just a bit. It is very easy, with inflammatory rhetoric, to create a sinister impression and interpretation of the whole Christian community. This is a terrible slander. I've spent the last thirty-five years working in prisons and with human rights groups. I've even earned the plaudits of Nicholas Kristoff, another *New York Times* columnist. Most of the Christians I know and see are well-meaning people who really bring a passion to human rights, and really want to be the best of citizens in the kingdom of man, because we love our God.

Let us never forget that the dominant principle governing our Western system of ethics is human dignity. It must be protected at all costs.

Our fevered critics in the media may not like to acknowledge it, but that was the most radical doctrine introduced into Western civilization when the Jews and Christians came out of the Middle East into the Greco-Roman Empire, and announced that all human beings were created equal in God's image. That didn't go over well with the Greeks or Romans, who had slaves and treated women as property.

We should be thanking God that there are those who carry on that tradition today, without which there'd be no system of ethics in the West.

# Hook-Up Culture

For half a century, we've watched the sexual emancipation of women on college campuses. It all started in the sixties with naked bodies groveling in the mud at Woodstock, and now this kind of behavior has become institutionalized. We have coed dorms, coed bathrooms—all restraints of shame and modesty are being removed.

The irony is that women led the charge. The feminists thought this was great: women could be "equal" to men, sexually speaking. It was the great liberation movement that would lead us to nirvana, freedom, equality.

So what is the result? A hook-up culture.

I know from talking to my grandkids, who just got out of college, that what used to be called "Animal House" a few decades ago, where men engaged in "the hunt" for women, was all a game. Today it's just like open hunting, no restrictions, no limits.

I've been waiting for the day feminists realize they have sold their own constituency down the river, because the only people who profit from this philosophy are men, who can now get all the sex they want—so why should they treat women with any dignity? They look at women as objects of gratification and pleasure—period. That's totally dehumanizing.

We've actually reverted to ancient Greek culture. The Greeks had no respect for women of any kind; they saw woman as property, to be used for their sexual gratification—basically as slaves. And the Christians burst on the scene with the radical doctrine that all human beings are created in the image of God, with innate dignity. And now we're right back to the attitude of the Greeks.

I've been waiting for someone to blow the whistle on it, and lo and behold, this week it happened. I saw a segment on NBC reporting that about a dozen Yale students filed a sexual harassment claim with the US Department of Education because of what has been going on at Yale. For instance, male students put out a directory of incoming freshman women called a "scouting report." It talked about their level of attractiveness and other details so the men would know who they should go after. The women also complained that some of the men were going by the women's dorms with suggestive chants.

What I found almost comical about this was how minor the so-called offenses were when you consider the sort of open, flagrant sexual environment of most college campuses today. And every time somebody objects to it, they say, wait a minute, you're interfering with our right to personal autonomy. So nobody is willing to blow the whistle on all this stuff. Certainly the men had no interest in doing so. But now some brave students at Yale have stepped forward. I could not help thinking, "What did you expect? Of course this was going to happen."

This is the ultimate postmodern impasse. We want total freedom; we want to be libertarians about what we do and who can tell us what to do. But then, all of a sudden, when it begins to hurt us and be untenable, then we scream. This is the problem with trying to have things both ways. This is the self-refuting nature of the postmodern social model. It doesn't work and it can't work.

But here's the second fascinating insight into this. When women blow the whistle, how do they go about it? Do they start a countermovement—say, a modesty movement? Do they try to invoke taboos and customs and fall back on prior generations' experiences, and try to create a cultural backlash? No, they go right to the government. We now want to have government tell us exactly what we can and cannot do.

I listened to the legal gobbledygook on the network. There will be a class action suit filed and two or three years of litigation. Somebody will get fined, and Yale will lose some federal benefits. That's what the penalty is for this.

But Yale can do nothing; they're powerless. These male students are just acting out what Yale has taught them is proper behavior. And not just Yale, practically every campus in the country, except, maybe, the Christian campuses.

But this leads to the very question I've been asking in speeches lately that really stops people in their tracks. Can freedom be maintained where virtue is not flourishing?

When you abandon all moral standards, you create chaos, and since there are no resources left to combat that chaos, no moral standard you can refer to in order to defend against it, then you go to the government. So what do you get?

Moral chaos will lead us to lose our freedoms. The inevitable consequence of the modern project of complete liberation from all restraints is slavery.

So Yale is giving us a look at what slavery is. It's going to an Ivy League school, paying $60,000 for a prestigious education, only to be sold into sexual bondage. And now, when we want to reverse this appalling moral catastrophe, we have to bring in Big Brother to tell us how to behave.

# The Marine Corps and the Christian Life

In the ethics series we're working on, I have been teaching that there are great parallels between achieving a virtuous life and the Marine Corps. Yes, I know, as a former Marine I'm obsessed with the Marine Corps, but I learned some of the greatest lessons of my life there.

What's necessary for a virtuous society is that people be transformed. That, of course, is the essence of the Christian life, isn't it? The old person dies; we go to the cross and leave the old self there and then take on the righteousness of Christ for the new self. That's the good news; Christ made this possible. It's not I who live but Christ who lives in me, for I've been crucified with Christ. For me, it's almost a life verse.

But how do you do this in the secular world? What we're teaching in the ethics course regards learning the virtues, pursing them, developing character, and forming conscience.

As I look around at American life today, at least in the secular arenas, the Marine Corps is the one place this is being done that I know of. Maybe also in the Army, Navy, and Air Force, but I know what happens in the Marines.

You go to boot camp, which is thirteen weeks, and in the first six weeks you are beaten to a pulp. The drill sergeant says you're lower than a worm. If you look at him the wrong way you do fifty push-ups. If he doesn't like the way you go over the obstacle course, you keep going over it until you faint (been there, done that).

At the end of six weeks, you feel utterly worthless. What they have done is strip away from you every bad habit you've ever had. They've made it impossible for you to think of yourself as you did before. You couldn't think very much of yourself; you have the absolute lowest esteem; it's gone so deep it's underground.

But in the last seven weeks, everything is aimed at building you up, teaching you that while you yourself have no worth, when you become a Marine, you do. And working together as a team, and all the things you're taught in the Marine Corps, if you can do that you can do anything.

There have been studies about some pretty messed-up kids—always in fights and drunken brawls—who go to boot camp. And when they go back home they are absolutely disgusted with the culture they were once a part of. They want nothing to do with it. It really shows how transforming that experience is.

But think about what it is: It's really a parallel with the gospel. There is no way that you can change a person without killing the old self and taking on a new life with different values and virtues. If you can apply that to preparing people who go into combat, why can't you apply that same methodology in life? Isn't that really what we're trying to do in Christian discipleship?

# Our Christian Heritage

I was fortunate enough to be invited to the dedication of the Marine Corps Museum at Quantico, a beautiful structure rising out of the Virginia countryside in a shape suggestive of the famous photo of the Marines raising the flag at Iwo Jima. While I sat waiting for the festivities to begin, I was struck as I looked around me at the incredible camaraderie that all of these Marines and former Marines enjoyed. An eighty-five-year-old man sitting right behind me said, "I've been a Marine for sixty-seven years." What he meant is what Marines say: once a Marine, always a Marine. He enlisted when he was eighteen, did his duty in the Pacific, came home, and built a life for himself. But here he was, halfway across the country, celebrating the opening of the Marine museum.

Jim Lehrer, the PBS newscaster and a former Marine, explained it well: "What's important to understand about Marines is that they know that their safety depends on the person on their right and the person on their left." You are bonded together in battle.

As I sat there on that beautiful autumn day with jets streaming overhead and flags waving, I was struck, not only by the beauty of what I was watching, the heritage being celebrated, but by a sort of envy. Why can't the church feel this way? Why can't we believe that our safety or our discipleship or our Christian faith depends upon the person on the left and the right? Do you think that when you look at the people in the pews around you?

During his talk, President George W. Bush introduced the parents of Jason Dunham, a young Marine corporal from upstate New York, born on November 10, the birthday of the Marine Corps. He was born, as Bush put it, to be a Marine. It was then announced that Dunham was being posthumously awarded the highest military honor that can be given: the Congressional Medal of Honor. Dunham had been leading a squad of Marines who were suddenly attacked. They were in hand-to-hand combat. An Iraqi militant seized Dunham by the neck, and Dunham shouted to his comrades, "Watch what he's got in his hand!" At which point the insurgent threw a live grenade into the midst of the Marines and released his grip on Dunham. The young man immediately turned and fell on his helmet over the grenade.

Why did he do it? To save the men serving under him: true heroic altruism—the one thing that Darwinian theories of natural selection can never account for. It's also the very thing the Bible calls Christians to be prepared to do: "Greater love has no one than this, to lay down one's life for one's friends" (John 15:13).

As part of the ceremony, the various battle flags of the Marines were paraded in front of the dais, starting with Tripoli, going through a score of names familiar to every Marine: Belleau Wood, Iwo Jima, Fallujah. The colors carried into the battle by the Marines were displayed. I don't think I was the only one in the crowd with my spine tingling, my chest swelling with just a little more pride. One of the things that drive Marines to be the best at their trade is their proud heritage. They know how important it is that they carry on that tradition.

I wonder how many Christians really understand the proud tradition of the faith: how the martyrs in the first century gave their lives to preserve the gospel; how Christians through the years have done the greatest works for the improvement of mankind; how William Wilberforce led the campaign against the slave trade and slavery itself. We all remember Mother Teresa, perhaps, but how about the saints of bygone years? How about the Christians in the Roman Empire who stayed to tend the sick when the pagan doctors fled in the great plagues—and many paid with their lives for it.

The story of human history is a great cosmic battle between good and evil. We're engaged in that battle on God's side. Would that we had the sense of loyalty and commitment and responsibility for heritage that I saw on exhibit in the faces of those proud Marines.

Nagging questions, these, in the midst of a glorious autumn day in Virginia.

# 5

# CRIME, PUNISHMENT, and JUSTICE

# Who Commits Crimes?

From the 1930s to the 1960s, we believed we could solve all the problems of crime by cleaning up the slums, getting rid of disadvantaged circumstances, and providing kids with a better education. We did this because we fell for the myth of the goodness of man. Then along came the conservatives and they really got tough on crime, thinking we could scare people out of committing crimes—but that didn't work, either.

The humanistic view of the conservatives, and I was one of them, was that offenders are rational calculators. They will sit down and decide that if the punishment is too great, they're not going to commit the crime. But things don't work that way; Romans 7 explodes that.[1] Two-thirds of crimes are committed under passion or under the influence of alcohol or drugs, so obviously, nobody has done any rational calculating.

The biblical view of justice is quite different. It actually embraces social justice—that is, helping people in need and seeing that they get what's due them. This is what liberals think, because we have all the injunctions in the Old Testament about paying a fair wage and taking care of the poor, and these carry over into the New Testament as well. Gleaning is a wonderful example in the Old Testament of true social justice where, if you plant a farm, you've got to leave crops on the side for the poor. But of course, the Bible is also filled with retributive justice—punishments, restitution, execution, and so on.

So Christians look at the question of justice in society and particularly preserving order and criminal justice. We're both liberals and conservatives; we cover the whole spectrum. We don't break it down and divide it the way the secular world does. But we see it in a broader sense, in terms of restoring *shalom*.

A Christian really is committed to finding the certainty of the laws. The whole idea of the rule of law is essential to a just society, and this is a clear Christian contribution, going back to the Decalogue and continuing through Samuel Rutherford. The Christian then sees the reality of a person being responsible for his own behavior because we're fallen creatures. We're sinful, not simply victims of society. We see that there's a way out because there's the moral reformation of the individual. And we see that there is a purpose to all of this, which is to bring about *shalom*. When you apply the worldview analysis to justice, you see how the Christian is really the only one who can come up with an enduring system of justice.

# The Bishop's Story

*Chuck could not tell the following story on* BreakPoint, *about an inmate named the Bishop, because he was afraid he would get so choked up he would be unable to finish the script.*

This is maybe the greatest single story I have heard of a Prison Fellowship volunteer and of an inmate's redemption.

Terry Van der Aa, a successful Chicago businessman, has been on our board and on our Wilberforce Advisory Committee for years. He went to Angola Prison in Louisiana, the biggest maximum security prison in the country. The visit totally transformed his life. He met warden Burl Cain, got involved with the inmates, and started going back regularly. He spent the day before Christmas at Angola—just bought a ticket and went down there. He went because he knew the inmates would have a tough time at Christmas. He's that kind of a guy.

In any event, in the course of things at Angola, he got to know a man called "the Bishop," a black inmate who had been sentenced for murder when he was twenty-three. His original sentence was the electric chair, but civil rights lawyers at Tulane discovered mishandling of the case—all the black jurors had been recused. So the Bishop had his conviction thrown out and reinstated as life without parole. He'd been at Angola fifty-one years. He was known as "the Bishop" because he was the leading Christian in the place.

The Bishop's conversion story is like that of the apostle Paul. He was in prison; he reconciled to the fact he would die there, and one night he just called out to God. At once he was transformed and knew Christ. It's just an incredible story. He became a leader inside Angola, building the church, which is one of the most amazing places in America because of what Burl Cain allowed the men to do.

No black inmate sentenced for murder and life without parole had ever been released from Angola—ever. But one day Terry had been down visiting the Bishop and some of the other inmates. In the guest house with Burl one night, he said, "You know, we've got to figure a way to get the Bishop out of here." So Burl and Terry mounted a campaign and got to Governor Kathleen Babineaux with a petition, and she turned it down. Burl went back to the governor and said, "Look, I've got a prison full of men who are there for life. If this guy, who is the best inmate in the place, can't get out, then they're going to know none of them will get out. They'll all die there. The place will become unmanageable. You've got to give people hope."

The governor refused to pardon the Bishop or cut his sentence to time served, but eventually agreed to reduce his sentence to fifty-four years, and then leave it to the parole board.

What the governor didn't know was that the Bishop had done four years before his sentence, so he'd been in prison fifty-five years. When the governor came back with the order, Burl never asked permission of anybody; he just checked with someone in the attorney general's office, and released the Bishop.

But he called Terry, who, knowing the Bishop was going to get out, had made arrangements with Jim Cymbala at the Brooklyn Tabernacle church for the Bishop to come there. Terry said, "I'll pay all his costs and give you a check every quarter—just tell me what his expenses are. I just want you to manage this guy and mentor him."

But Jim wasn't ready to take him. So Terry flew down to Baton

Rouge with his pastor, met the Bishop in prison, and took him to the airport. The Bishop had never flown in his life; he'd seen nothing of the world for fifty-four years; he was almost eighty years old. Just think of the changes that had happened! The Bishop was wide-eyed as he looked around him.

They got to the airport to find the flight was oversold and there was a weight problem—it was a small plane going to Chicago. The three men were told they couldn't get on. The ticket agent, after some discussion, looked over at the Bishop and said, "Aren't you the Bishop?"

"Yes," the Bishop answered.

The ticket agent said, "I just became a Christian. I heard you speak in the prison one night."

The agent then went to speak with her manager, and when she came back, she said, "You three will be on the plane."

After they landed, Terry had no place to put the Bishop. What would you or I do? I'd put him at the Salvation Army or somewhere he could get on his feet. Terry didn't do that. He took the Bishop to his beautiful home in the suburbs. He stayed there for nine days. Terry took him out to get clothes and all the legal documents he needed, and sort of indoctrinated him to life on the outside.

By then Jim Cymbala was ready for him, so Terry took the Bishop to Brooklyn, where he now lives in an apartment. He is something of a celebrity in his church. The way he was received at Brooklyn Tabernacle is a story in itself. When he walked in the front door, the choir sang him a hymn about being home. Terry's a pretty stern Dutchman, but he said he'd never shed so many tears in his life. It was the most joyous thing he'd ever been a part of.

This story is what Prison Fellowship Ministries is about. If somebody asked me for my legacy, I'd say Terry Van der Aa and the Bishop. It so incredibly illustrates what we do.

# "We're Scoopers Too"

The meeting in Philadelphia on September 15, 2000, was a grand moment in the history of Prison Fellowship. Thirteen pastors of inner-city churches joined at Herb Lusk's Greater Exodus Baptist Church.

Herb is a remarkable guy. He was at the peak of his career as a running back with the Philadelphia Eagles when he felt God's call. At the beginning of a season he shocked the sports world by announcing his retirement so that he could attend seminary. Then he took over a church that had about a dozen members right on the edge of the projects in the worst part of Philadelphia. He built that into an absolutely magnificent ministry. He took over the entire block and now has a sanctuary that has been remodeled and that is full all the time. He has a very active outreach in the community, working with kids and feeding the hungry. He is a no-nonsense, solid evangelical who is getting people out of welfare into work, out of despair into the hope of the gospel. He's a natural leader.

It would be hard to find a group of people who could preach as powerfully and passionately as the people who came to that meeting. The mayor may have stolen the show, confessing as he did that government simply can't solve social problems, that government needs the faith-based communities. He pledged to work with all of the faith-based programs present. It was a great, powerful message.

Eugene Rivers, pastor of Azusa Christian Community, was there from Boston and did a superb job talking about what could be done with the faith community. The former mayor of Philadelphia, Reverend W. Wilson Goode, gave a beautiful talk, as did John Dilulio and Luis Lugo along with Senator Dan Coats, who spoke powerfully for Big Brothers, Big Sisters, and other groups.

It was a joy for me to be sitting on the platform looking out over a crowd of blacks and whites, rich and poor, and many ex-convicts. I looked to my left and saw Rich DeVos, one of the leading businessmen in America; I looked over to the second pew and saw Jack Donahue, another of America's most prominent financial leaders sitting with his family. I looked at the children's choir from one of the local churches. And there was a group of kids from Camden, one of the worst ghettos in America, who had taken part in Angel Tree camps, and who were absolutely marvelous. Looking out over the deeply diverse crowd, I was struck with the realization that only God could produce this. And only God could use something as simple as Angel Tree for such powerful ends. Over the past decades, the program has grown to reach half a million kids.

I also thought of Mary Kay Mahaffey, now Mary Kay Beard, a prisoner coming out of prison after eight years, a former safe cracker and bank robber, appointed as an area director for Prison Fellowship. Angel Tree was Mary Kay's idea. She had a burden for children of prisoners. She moved ahead in faith, had a wonderfully inspired idea, made it work, and look what God has done with it. You don't have to be big and powerful to make things happen in the world; you just have to be faithful and let a sovereign God work through you.

We had a chance to mingle with eight kids who'd attended Angel Tree Camp after the service, and it was wonderful talking to them. While I chatted with them a black woman, perhaps in her late forties or early fifties, reached across the rail and tapped me on the shoulder. "Oh, Mr. Colson," she said. "I am so grateful to you and to Angel Tree and Prison Fellowship. My little grandson went to your camp last summer and he was saved. Now he's out on the streets reading the Bible to people and evangelizing." She had tears in her eyes while she told me this.

Then I talked to her grandson, who was a fine young man, maybe twelve or thirteen. He clearly had come to love God and wanted to preach. Looking at this little guy's eyes, I realized that he was a kid who might well have been lost, might well have followed in the path of his father and ended up in prison. Instead, he was getting mentored and was evangelizing other kids.

That is Angel Tree. It is the real reward all of us who have worked with this program receive.

The potential for this program is absolutely limitless. Frank Lofaro tells us that 75 percent of all kids at risk live in roughly twenty urban areas. In a matter of a few years we could have an outreach with the potential of reaching 70 percent of the kids most at risk in America. No one else has been able to do anything like this; it would be an incredible breakthrough.

The fact is, we are in a unique position to do this. We know who these kids are, and we get to them at Christmastime by invitation of their parents. We visit them on behalf of their incarcerated parents. We share the gospel with them. We have an opportunity right then to match them up with a mentor. And then it's a matter of feeding them into after-school programs and into summer camp. We'll know in due course how many of those kids can be rescued, but even getting 10 to 15 percent of them would have enormous social and political ramifications in America.

The whole country would have to look at what is happening in the streets of the inner cities, and see Christians out of inner-city churches and suburban churches alike working with these kids and literally rescuing them, scooping them up off the streets. I announced that day that's what we were going to do, and that while the streets had been owned by the drug dealers and the pimps and the gangs, watch out, because the Christians are coming—the people of God—and we're going to scoop these kids up and rescue them from the streets.

The crowd really responded. The *Philadelphia Enquirer* picked up on that line. And some people came up at the dinner that night to say, "We're just scoopers like you."

Driving to the Great Exodus Baptist Church was a real experience. We went by the projects, which are incredibly dismal, many of them boarded up now. These apparently are the worst streets in all of Philadelphia, and this was precisely where we have now planted the flag, right in what was once the gang stronghold of the city.

God's people are marching. Several years ago in Philadelphia we began the invasion. It was a D-Day. Victory is in sight.

# Reckless Abandon

I went to New York for the Evangelicals and Catholics Together meetings, which were excellent, but as so often happens, God gave me an unexpected and very rich blessing in the process.

Jose Abreu, who has one of the most dazzling testimonies I've heard, and his wife, Mayra, who works on Angel Tree full-time out of the New York office, asked if they could pick me up at LaGuardia and drive me to the hotel. I accepted the offer because I love them and wanted to have a few minutes to talk with them in the car.

When we met at the airport, I discovered that they had not had dinner, so we found a hash house in Queens and all of us piled in for a meal — Jose, Mayra, their daughter, and three little boys. We had an absolutely great time.

Jose and Mayra live in a three-bedroom apartment in a public housing project, but they have just been approved for a Habitat for Humanity house in Queens. For the first time since Jose was in prison, they're going to be homeowners, and they are really excited about it.

The three little African American boys with them are all children abandoned by their mothers, prisoners at Riker's Island. Jose and Mayra, who have nothing, have always opened their home to abandoned kids. In fact, they pretty well staff the nursery at Riker's Island, so they are able to place kids whose mothers are in prison or take them themselves. Their house is always full.

I was so proud of this family at dinner, listening to them talk about the Lord, listening to Mayra tell me about all the great work that's being done on Angel Tree follow-up in New York.

It was a divinely ordained evening for me, because I needed it so badly — but also for Jose. We had gotten to the restaurant late, when it was half empty, and taken a table in the corner. I was sure this was one place I'd never be recognized, a little diner in Queens, New York, surrounded by tenements and row houses. I was wrong.

The man at the next table looked over at me, dropped his chin, and came over to introduce himself. He was an African American man who handles Christian celebrities. He couldn't believe he had found Chuck Colson sitting with a Hispanic family in a diner in Queens. Jose is looking for a job, and this man had an associate looking for someone with Jose's talents. They arranged to meet the next day.

As Christian leaders, we can go to board meetings and do strategy sessions and raise money and give speeches and attend justice conferences, but in the final analysis, prison ministry is all about people like Jose and Mayra. They are real Christians, not the kind of folks who dress up on Sunday morning and go to the most beautiful church, but people who live out their faith in every way you can imagine. God used us in prison ministry as His instruments in redeeming Jose and Mayra, and now they in turn are working with hundreds of others. And I needed an evening to be with people who really love God and are willing to follow Him with reckless abandon.

I share this story to encourage you. Great ministry is going on, and all across America there are families like the Abreus who are doing the gospel. God is good.

# Utopian Notions

I once visited a prison in Norway that I found incredibly sterile. It was a one-story building that looked more like a schoolhouse than a prison. There were no guard towers, yards, and that sort of thing on the outside. It was sitting on a fairly open area some miles out of Oslo. It wouldn't be the kind of place that would draw any attention.

Inside, however, was totally different. The walls were white, and there was almost an antiseptic, clinical feeling to the place. In its brightness, neatness, and sterility it was terribly oppressive.

That won't seem logical to people who think of prisons as dark holes, with slimy floors, rattling cells, and steel bars—oppressive places. But the reverse was you felt like you were in a laboratory, and you were the laboratory animal. That's quite oppressive. That's just what this felt like, and of course that's the way they treat the inmates: that they are not sinful, they haven't done terrible things; they're just poor people who have a mental imbalance.

And they are sentenced to the prison not for punishment, that is, not with a determinate sentence, but rather until they can be cured. All I could think of walking through this prison was that incredibly good essay by C. S. Lewis, the "Humanitarian Theory of Punishment," when he talks about Viennese scientists in white coats hovering over the poor subjects to cure them in laboratories, and that's just what this was. Because the Norwegian justice system doesn't believe in the fall, or the sin of man, they have to view this terrible behavior as an aberration. Therefore, they put people who commit crimes in prison until they can "cure" them.

What was missing in the prison were smiles, laughter, or even anger. In American prisons you will find some yelling and shouting, but you won't find the deadness, the hollow souls of the people that sort of drifted through this prison and these huge white doors with glass windows that are opened with locks, and then people move silently from one room to the next. It was like seeing apparitions float by, and it was deadening.

In the chapel I got very little emotion out of anybody. They sat there like they were drugged, and maybe they were. In a lot of prisons, the mentally ill are kept drugged so that they are easy to handle.

The telling moment was when a correctional officer came up to me, a woman in her early to mid-twenties, very attractive and very Nordic with blue eyes and blond hair. She was so excited; she said that she had been in the prison for several years and had never heard the gospel, and it was proclaimed so clearly that day that she was joyous. She said that's what these men needed to hear and they needed to take responsibility for their behavior and they needed to be transformed by Christ. She was marvelous.

I learned a few days later that this lovely correctional officer had taken an inmate to the theater, which was a part of keeping him normal, and on the way to or from he had assaulted and killed her.

These are the consequences of the denial of sin: the kind of institution I saw in Scandinavia and then of course the kind of tragedies that can flow from it.

The price of not recognizing the reality of sin is that we actually magnify it and make it worse. We increase the dangers of the reality of evil because we refuse to acknowledge it, refuse to hold people accountable for it, and perversely encourage it.

How did we ever get into this fix? What caused us to believe this myth that we're basically good?

I always go back to Rousseau, because he so outrageously argued that children are really born good, that they are corrupted only by the structures of society, and that the job of society is to create the kind of structures that will set people free. Remember, he said that the state should force people to be free.

This was a very popular view in French culture in the middle of the eighteenth century, part of the emerging belief in the independence of man leading to the French Revolution, and then was built upon by Enlightenment thinkers. It became one of the cardinal principles of the anti-God movement. If God is out of the picture, we don't need Him to explain creation; we don't need Him for the formulation of moral values. People are basically good. Who needs to be restrained by God; who needs a Savior?

But of course this directly feeds utopianism. This is the pretense that humanity is good, and therefore, if the elite construct a free society, well, then people will live in a perfect paradise thereafter. This line of reasoning from Rousseau, mediated by Nietzsche and Marx and Freud and others, resulted in Stalin, Hitler, Pol Pot, and the other tyrants of the twentieth century. It is no coincidence that Pol Pot was reading Rousseau as he was sending people off to the killing fields.

At another level in America this line of thinking led to a softer form of despotism, the idea that we could create a Great Society, that people could be programmed — that is, socially engineered into paradise by the right structuring of society.

Even though we're now seeing the flaws of the Great Society and disassembling it, we will not be able to erase the consequences of the utopian notion that we can create the perfect society, that people are not responsible for their behavior so that all we have to do is condition them properly, and the impact all of that has had in eroding personal responsibility.

In the era I know best I've seen this up close, and it's ugly. Ramsey Clark in the sixties said poverty is the cause of crime. Lyndon Johnson told people in the cities that he understood why they lived in such deprived environments. Hubert Humphrey, then vice president, said if he were living in slums, he'd revolt too. Jimmy Carter in the late seventies, talking about the looting that took place in New York after an electrical blackout, said that obviously the people were doing this because they were poor. A study later showed that most of them were not on welfare and most of them didn't take things they needed.

But the sum total of all this political rhetoric was to tell people that they weren't really bad, they weren't really misbehaving, they weren't morally defective. Instead, they were victims of a society that had been unjust and racist, and they'd been forced to stay in their poverty.

There has been a 600 percent increase in crime since the sixties, since we firmly implanted in the minds of people that they really weren't responsible for their behavior, that if they were criminals, they weren't at fault but were simply victims of an unjust society, and it was the government's job to fix it all.

Not only has this, in my opinion at least, been at the root of the surge in crime, it has also been responsible for all sorts of social dysfunctions and pathologies. Not the least of these is the fact that nobody feels responsible for anything.

The Menendez brothers in the late 1980s shot their own parents and then claimed they were abused. Some burglar breaks into a building, hurts himself, and sues the company he was trying to steal from for failing to maintain proper safety standards. A doctor is arrested for drunken driving, kicks the policeman, kicks the breathalyzer across the street, and then gets off because she tells the judge she was suffering from premenstrual syndrome. Serial killers can be forgiven because they had deprived childhoods.

Really, our culture believes that the problem is that people are deprived, not depraved. But in removing the moral component, that is, our responsibility for our own behavior, we have compounded sin.

The story about what happened in the Norwegian prison is a parable for what has happened in our culture at large.

The loss of the notion that we are responsible moral agents and that we do wrong things for which we need to be restrained or punished when we do them has created social chaos.

This has profoundly affected the church. It affects us both because we've been suckered into it—we want to think the best of people; it's easy for the church to fall into this trap—but also it takes all the edge out of our evangelization. If people are good, who really needs a Savior? How can we come to terms with Christ until we understand our own sin and our need for a Savior?

The biblical doctrine of the sinfulness of man—and therefore the need for God and a Savior—was dispensed with in the Enlightenment. Basically, eighteen centuries of rather settled thought in the West came unglued in the French Revolution and its wake.

# Advice to a Presidential Candidate

*While Chuck refused to engage in partisan politics, he never turned down a request for advice. What follows is Chuck's answer to a recent presidential campaign's question about how best to approach crime and punishment.*

We can't do anything with the crime problem until we understand the cause of it. Sociologists always thought it was environment, poverty, race, etc. But a psychiatrist and a psychologist in the mid-seventies completed a seventy-one-year longitudinal study, and contrary to their expectations, they discovered that crime is caused by wrong moral choices, and the answer is the "conversion" of the offender to a responsible lifestyle.[2] These weren't Christians; they were both Jewish. The "conversion" term merely means your life has got to be turned around morally.

The second definitive study came in the eighties. Professors Wilson and Hernnstein at Harvard discovered that crime was caused by the lack of moral training during morally formative years.[3]

If this is true, then big institutions aren't going to be able to solve the problem. We're going to have to do something about reinstilling family values in American life and policies to encourage healthy family life for kids. Working for the past thirty-two years in prisons, as I have, I know the overwhelming majority of prisoners are from broken homes, with no father figure. Psychologist Wade Horn's work here is very definitive.[4]

So one initiative certainly could be prevention for juveniles. A lot of states have tried some good alternatives through pretrial intervention programs, putting young offenders to work rather than into prison. The second thing that can be done is to mentor kids. They get into gangs because that's how they develop their peer relationships. But mentors can break that and get them into different kinds of relationships. Either faith-based or volunteer community groups ought to be mentoring at-risk kids. It's low-cost, and it's extremely effective.

The next thing we can do is help families while the husbands are incarcerated. Once again we should call on the church and volunteer community to reach out to these families. We have a program called Angel Tree, which has reached about 8.5 million people since we started it twenty-five years ago. We take the kids gifts at Christmas, mentors pick the kids up, and often send them to summer camp.

We can also do a lot to encourage visiting and phone calls so that the family is kept together while one of the parents is in prison.

The biggest item, however, is the recidivism statistics. Within three years, 50 percent of released prisoners are rearrested and put back in prison. This tells us that we do not have a good reentry system, because 95 percent of law enforcement resources are on the front end, catching and incarcerating criminals. Then we do nothing except shoo them out the front gate, and they nearly all come back. Surprise, surprise.

Most of the failures occur soon after the inmate is released. Old friends tempt him; he doesn't find a job; he's got no place to turn. He's got all kinds of excuses, and he falls back into the old ways.

Again, mentoring relationships are the answer. The Second Chance Act recommended by President Bush and passed by the Senate and House was a tremendous step forward. We need to involve the faith-based and community agencies to help.

A study was finished in 2003 by the University of Pennsylvania measuring the graduates of Prison Fellowship programs who had mentors and had been at least two years in our in-prison programming. The recidivism rate was cut to 8 percent compared to 20 percent with a control group. But when the mentor component was added, it was cut to 4 percent. We are operating facilities in nine states where this is working, daily.

It's all well and good to get tough on crime and lock people up. But if we don't do anything with them, when they're back out on the streets, they're going to reoffend. And this is a big national problem. The prison and jail population today is 2.3 million; 600,000 will be released this year—that's three times the size of the United States Marine Corps, and 50 percent will end up right back in prison.

The system can be fixed, but only if we put resources into effectively reintegrating people into society, and then do something about gang culture that has swept up our kids off the streets. It's not hard to know what to do; it's hard to get the will to do it.

# A Sense of Joy

It was, as always, a great day going into Florida prisons with Operation Starting Line, a volunteer prison visitation outreach of Prison Fellowship Ministries. Last week we spent the afternoon in the faith-based prison at Lawtey. The chaplain is a former Prison Fellowship area director, and PF churches play a big role in that prison.

When I preached in the yard to a really good crowd of inmates, I had the most wonderful sensation. Looking out over the sea of inmates and the people dressed in yellow jerseys (the Starting Line volunteers), I couldn't help but think of how far God had brought us since the first days of this ministry over thirty years ago. All we had thirty years ago were three or four paid employees, a big vision, a little rented office, and not much money in the bank.

Looking at the faces of that crowd it struck me that God had answered our earliest prayers. That yard full of inmates knew we cared for them. When Larry Howard asked how many had heard of Angel Tree, over half the hands went up. And when he mentioned *Inside Journal*, our newspaper for inmates, even more went up. And of course our volunteers are in that prison regularly.

I realized how good God has been to fulfill the earliest vision; He has not just been good to us, but also good to the inmates. What drove me to go back into the prisons when I finished my sentence was the realization that nobody cared for these people, that they were really forgotten members of our society, and that the prisons were broken. Now, thirty years later, I got a glimpse that day of what is happening all over America and all over the world. I had goose bumps up my back as I was preaching.

I gave a different message that day and talked about God using the broken people in prison to raise up a new generation of leaders for his church.

After I'd spoken and mingled with the inmates, several mentioned that I had given them great hope. Two or three said what I've heard thousands of times in prisons, "I never thought my life could amount to anything, but maybe it can." There's probably no refrain I've heard more often in prison yards than that. These men come from broken homes, battered relationships; they've been beaten down and thrown in a prison and told they're no good—don't complain. You did the crime now you've got to do the time. But we come along and give them hope.

The one thing that Prison Fellowship's building in Lansdowne, Virginia, and our ongoing ministry, and the success of people who've graduated from our programs, and ex-offenders who've come back to work in the ministry represents, is hope. Our ministry seeks to show them that they're not good for nothing. They can make something of their lives. They can be used by God. They can accomplish great things.

I didn't have any blinding new revelations that day, just an affirmation that our vision is right, that God is leading us. I also felt an overwhelming sense of joy that I could see, at long last, men and women—who'd thought they were forgotten and had no hope in life and would never make anything of themselves—who now had real hope. How gracious God has been.

The next morning we toured death row and the disciplinary cells, doing cell-to-cell ministry. I ran into two inmates who were really quite remarkable, each in his own way.

The first one was named Leonardo. He was a Cuban who'd come to this country in the Mariel boat lift. His uncle had been in prison for eighteen years as a political prisoner of Castro, and his father had been in prison as well.

Leonardo, it turned out, had been on death row for fifteen years. He must have been getting near a final decision in his case. I really couldn't believe it when he told me he'd been imprisoned fifteen years because his mind was so sharp, he was so keen, and he was so in love with the Lord. We talked about books—he'd read them all. We talked about Scripture, doctrine, and faith. This guy was as mature a disciple as I've run into anywhere in a prison—and far more mature than the typical Christian layperson that I know.

Fifteen years in a solitary cell would drive most men mad. But this guy was vibrant and alive in his faith. It just shows what a person can do under incredibly adverse conditions. In fact, you might say because of the conditions, instead of in spite of them. I realized once again that when everything else is stripped away, when we have no other idols in life, when it's nothing but Jesus and us in that prison cell, the mind is incredibly focused. There are no distractions.

I don't know what happened to this brother. We had a wonderful time of prayer together. But if he ever gets out of that death row cell, he's going to be a powerhouse. He is a natural leader—articulate, smart, quick, and extremely bright.

The second inmate that impressed me very much was Monty. Monty is a strong believer with an incredible writing gift. He read me some of his poems, which he said he was going to submit to *Inside Journal*. They were outstanding—very well crafted and with very powerful messages. He was in the disciplinary lockup because he had written a poem to one of the nurses, which of course broke all kinds of rules.

Monty told me that he'd been on crack cocaine, that he had been a complete bum, drifting around in Ft. Lauderdale, before eventually getting arrested. I think he's doing a relatively short sentence, maybe three years, and is going to need a lot of help when he gets out so he doesn't go back on drugs. But he's a gifted man, also very attractive and articulate, and very, very mature in his faith.

It was a great day, and it reminded me of how gracious God has been to Prison Fellowship, how beautiful it is to see its vision becoming fulfilled, and how much I love the ministry. Just think, all across the country there are people like Monty and Leonardo and all those guys in the prison yard that day.

# The Real Causes of Crime

There was very good news on the crime front last year. New York City ended 2009 with 466 murders—the lowest number since records have been kept.

Other statistics showed crime in every category dropping dramatically. Homicide in Los Angeles was down 25 percent; car thefts were down nearly 20 percent. And similar reports were coming in from all across America.

What's the explanation? Have police gotten smarter? Have more resources been put into prisons and punishment? No, quite to the contrary. Prison budgets have been slashed. Police, like everyone else, have had to absorb huge budget cuts in the recession.

But wait a minute; something doesn't add up. For generations, the liberal theory has been that the cause of crime is poverty. Ramsey Clark, Lyndon Johnson's attorney general in the sixties, said exactly that. Yet in 2009, the economy had tanked in the greatest recession since the 1930s. The only way to explain this seeming contradiction is to understand the root causes of crime, and the false worldviews that Americans have been buying over the last several generations.

The Christian worldview tells us that man is responsible for his own behavior, that the cause of crime in the world is original sin. Human beings are not morally neutral; they are disposed towards sin.[5] Therefore, crime is, as one Jewish psychiatrist said in the seventies, the result of people making wrong moral choices.

If this is the case, then individuals, not society, are responsible for human behavior.

But this introduces the concepts of sin and human responsibility. There are no more politically incorrect terms. How judgmental of us to talk about the sinful behavior of people! They're only causing all these problems because they had a bad environment, sucked their thumbs too long, had a dysfunctional childhood, or are victims of racism and poverty. So went the conventional liberal wisdom through most of the twentieth century.

What happened in 2009? The same thing that happened during the Great Depression in the 1930s. Crime fell during tough economic times because the whole societal attitude shifted. In tough times, people have a natural inclination to try to help one another, not to rob each other. That may sound simplistic, but it's true. Tough times build stronger communities and actually encourage more responsible individual behavior.

The eminent social scientist, James Q. Wilson, discovered in a far-ranging survey of American crime statistics, that during tough economic times, crime receded. During boom times, it increased. Counterintuitive? Yes, to today's liberal mind.

But Christians understand it perfectly well. People are fallen by nature. They're restrained only by their consciousness of the law.

If young kids see conspicuous consumption promoted in popular culture, they're more likely to commit criminal acts. We're really not pawns of society; we really are responsible, moral agents.

Where do you find that? In the Christian worldview. This is just another example of what happens when society buys a lie instead of the truth. Just another example of why it is so imperative for each one of us to be advancing a Christian view of all of life—and as I know so well from decades of experience, nowhere is this more important than in the criminal justice field.

# The Camel's Nose

I recently saw on Fox News a very interesting report from Los Angeles. The police department there had received a $3 million grant from the federal government to use crime statistics to try to calculate where future crimes were going to be committed. The theory behind this was that if you can show a pattern in certain geographical areas, then you would be able to predict where crimes would occur and would put more resources there.

On the surface that sounds efficient, smart, and an intelligent use of computers. And it is, if that's as far as you take it. But you know what the next step would be—trying to identify the blocks of people who are most likely to commit those crimes. So what you would do is have the police patrolling areas they expect crimes to occur in. And pretty soon you would get to the point of trying to predict the behavior of those people who were going to commit the crimes.

That can lead to the stuff of a police state. The idea of preventative detention, and we do get into that somewhat with sex offenders, has been a concern of civil liberties groups. So if I were in the ACLU I would be howling over this study in California. It is the camel's nose under the tent ... and we should be on top of these kinds of issues.

# 6

# HAPPINESS

# Inexpressible Joy

If we really understand the great promise that one's eternal destiny is settled with Christ, that understanding alone frees us from the tyranny of the moment, today's passion, tomorrow's greed.

I have discovered a real freedom from the desires I had earlier in my life for money and power. At least, I'm a lot better than I used to be. When you're freed from these things, you can truly enjoy relationships. You also no longer look at people in a utilitarian way. You don't befriend someone because he or she can make you rich.

I realized that while riding home with a cab driver from Ghana the other night. He got so excited when he recognized me, and although I was tired and in a hurry, I stayed downstairs when he dropped me at my apartment and talked with him about his life. He got his camera out and we stopped some of the people coming into the building to take pictures. But I really got a thrill over talking to him about what God has done in his life, and the cab driver can never do anything for me. That is, I had nothing to gain by spending time with him.

I'm also nervous in my relationships with some of the wealthier supporters of Prison Fellowship, wondering whether I like to spend time with them because they're major donors or because they are who they are. I don't think I've gotten where I should be, yet, but I'm getting there. I just enjoy people for the relationships.

When Christ says the truth will set you free, I think this is part of the freedom that He's talking about. And it's not something you have earlier in life when you're trying to build an enterprise or accumulate your retirement. I was just realizing this the other day when Dallen Peterson called me. He was almost giddy. He said he was thinking a lot over the weekend and the truth came through to him that nothing he has belongs to him; it all belongs to God. He said he had been holding on to stock and waiting for it to go up before he made his charitable gifts and he had been calculating what he had. It just hit him all of a sudden, over the weekend, that he wanted to be totally free and didn't even want to think about that. If he gave it all away, and there was nothing left, it wasn't any different from before when he didn't have anything, so why was he allowing wealth and money to influence him?

The things that I think about now, looking at life through the rearview mirror, the things that give me total joy, are the experiences I've had either helping my kids or helping other people. I remember going to Buckingham Palace for the Templeton Prize. It was a wonderful experience, and of course, a great honor, but I don't think back on that very often. And when I do, I don't get goose bumps over it. I've been back to the White House on several occasions now, and it's always a great experience, and of course, I enjoy it, but it doesn't set my heart skipping or beating faster. I can't even remember all of the honorary doctorates I've received or the prizes or awards over the years.

When I look at my life in its full sweep, what I realize is that the only things that really give me sustained joy—indeed, the kind of inexpressible joy that the apostle Paul talks about—have to do with the people I've helped: the men in the prisons I've introduced to Christ, and the people who tell me that one of my books has changed their lives, or that my testimony saved their marriage.

My service in the Marines is a particularly gratifying memory, not just because of the pride of the Marine Corps and not just because I enjoyed what I did, but also because military service is truly altruistic service. You're prepared to lay down your life for something you believe in deeply: your countrymen. This is the right kind of patriotism. You care about how other people live so you're willing to sacrifice yourself for them.

These are the kinds of things I think about as I grow older, and the kinds of things that give me true happiness. The only things that really give you any sense of fulfillment are what you've been able to do for others.

I think this applies to giving, as well. I think the things that we're going to look back on with pleasure, as we reflect on our lives, is how we've enabled others to have better lives. Patty and I support a child through World Vision. I think about him a lot, and how much fun it is to think that we're helping him get an education and do something worthwhile with his life, and that he can know Christ.

Even the secularist, however, is going to get some enjoyment out of this. If you donate money to build an art museum, for instance, people are going to come and enjoy that art. Beauty is an absolute, as the Greeks saw it, and as I see it. Helping people to appreciate art, and giving them an experience at the museum that lifts their spirits, is something that ennobles them. You might endow a chair even at some liberal university, which is a dumb thing for anybody with any sense to do, but even this is going to enable students to learn. So donors can get great satisfaction out of giving.

Does it matter that you had a sports car you really enjoyed driving? Does it matter how many rounds of golf you played, or how many trophies you put on your shelf, or how many degrees you've hung on the wall? Not at all. What really counts is what you're enabled to do to enrich another's life.

It's also true that the bad things we do carry with them their own punishment. So there are rewards and punishments in everything. The reward is knowing that we're doing something to help someone else; the bad is that we have to live with the regrets, when we survey our lives, and see the tears we brought into the lives of others.

All of this makes sense if you stop and realize that two of the great capitals of the world, Washington and London, are but brick and mortar; they're cities. One day all of the grand buildings in these cities will resemble the ruins in Athens and Rome. But the soul is eternal; it goes on forever. Therefore, what we do for the human soul is incomparably more important than what we do for the transient things of this world. This is why so many writers—T. S. Eliot chief among them—talked about the society of permanent things—that is, the values and enduring qualities of life. These are the things that really count.

I think the key question that I ask myself as the years fly by is: Have I kept faith with God's purposes in my life?

Many kids want more than anything to please their parents.

When you look back on life, the big question is: Have you pleased your Father who is in heaven?

# I'm Happy, You're Not

I just read an interesting article on Tony Blair. He will soon retire as prime minister of England, around the same time George W. Bush enters his last year as president here in America. Things are really pretty good in both Britain and America. Our democracies are strong, our economies are vibrant [this was before the economic crisis really came to light]. So why are the leaders of both nations personally vilified, almost detested? This article suggests that Brits are generally hard on their politicians. That to me is pure nonsense.

I think there are two factors behind it, both of which deserve a biblical worldview perspective. One is, the more people have, the angrier they get. Witness the fact that America is regarded as one of the most unhappy nations on earth, according to recent studies. We take more tranquilizers than any other people, and yet we have an extremely high standard of living. The happiest people, according to the same survey, turned out to be Nigerians, who have one of the lowest standards of living.

The problem is, we are spoiled rotten. We've got everything we could possibly want. But we're not happy and we don't know why, so we get angry at everybody else. Over the span of the last twenty-five years, I've noticed a difference in the way people behave. There's a lot more anger.

For instance, ten days ago a guy on a plane punched me in the arm because the guy next to me had his cell phone out. I was sitting in the aisle, and the guy at the window had his cell phone out. The guy across the aisle whacked me on the arm. I told him afterward, "You know, it's a good thing I'm a Christian, because I'm a former Marine, pretty good at judo, and I'm an ex-con. If I weren't a Christian you might have been flat on the floor of this plane."

People just get angry. On the plane they were shouting at each other and screaming across me.

What in the world is wrong with us?

The second problem is that we have politicized everything. We think nothing is going to happen that isn't proposed in Washington, argued about by the talking heads at night, and then voted on, and if they can't deliver, then we knew that we should have thrown the bums out anyway. If you once get the notion in your head that there's a political solution to everything, and you don't have to do anything except let those people take care of everything for you, you will eventually be controlled by those people. But in the meantime, government will get so big and cumbersome it can't even function. And that's the point we're at.

# Sinking Spirits

According to an article I read in the *New York Times,* violent crime is rising sharply in cities, reversing a downward trend. And this is happening as unemployment seems to be at an all-time low.

This should convince us that there is no connection between the economy and crime, violent or otherwise. The country is in a boom, yet people are killing each other.

The problem, of course, is sin. But why is it being aggravated today? Is it because of violence on TV, or in the movies? Perhaps. Or maybe it's just a totally self-absorbed culture that makes us believe that everything should be done the way we want it to be done when we want it to be done, and we're entitled to everything life can give us. We don't want to wait for anything. Deferred gratification is a lost virtue. We want it, and we want it now. If somebody gets in our way, get rid of him.

I've seen more road rage and anger in the last couple of years than I ever remember before. Maybe I just don't remember it, but it really seems to have gotten bad. In traffic the other day, I pulled out of a lane, a little close to the guy behind me, who was in a small car; to be honest I didn't really see him clearly. He blasted his horn, and that was okay. I got back in my lane. But that wasn't enough. The other driver pulled alongside me and shook his fist at me. Then, about three blocks later, when I started to turn off, he blasted his horn again at me. There seems to be a lot of anger out there because people want their way and don't want anybody else in their way.

I'm sure a lot of the violence is drug- and gang-related, but I'm sure a lot of it is passion as well. We know that about 60 percent of homicides take place among people who knew each other well.

After reading the *New York Times* that day, I turned to the *Wall Street Journal*, where my eye was caught by an article titled "Richest Country, Saddest People. Any Coincidence?"[1] It was the De Gustibus column by Bret Stephens, and he pointed out that America is the richest country on earth, but has the saddest people. That is, we had the highest rate of depression among a survey group of fourteen countries.

The study was conducted by the World Health Organization and Harvard Medical School, and was based on more than sixty thousand interviews worldwide. It found that 9.6 percent of Americans suffer from bipolar disorder, major depressive disorders, or chronic minor depression; 18.2 percent of Americans were also found to experience mood and anxiety disorders. This is staggering, the consummation of the Prozac nation.

What do these statistics about rising crime and sinking spirits have in common? Money and wealth do not buy happiness or free us from crime. It's not the economy, stupid.

In fact, counterintuitive as it may seem, the more possessions we have, the more things we want to acquire. The more consumer driven our economy is, the unhappier we are, because we can never be satisfied with things. As Christians we know that to be true. But the secular world doesn't.

In fact, these two articles had something in common. People get angry and depressed enough to have wild mood swings. They are also killing each other more often. Is that really surprising? As Stephens argued in his article, if your sole goal in life is finding a place to sleep and enough food for your family, that's really all you think about. It's only when you're faced with this constant pressure to accumulate more things that you start getting depressed, and in the more extreme cases, begin killing people.

# Healthy Guilt

Hayes Wicker, my pastor at First Baptist Church in Naples, Florida, recently preached a great message. He talked about how the closer one gets to God, the more one is aware of his or her own sin. This is really true: the more one desires holiness, the more one is confronted by one's own sinfulness. If you're not thinking about your own sinfulness, it's because you aren't thinking enough of God's graciousness. It's a great paradox among the many paradoxes of the Christian faith.

This means that guilt is not a neurosis; it's a healthy emotion, the response of an offended conscience which drives one back to the foot of the cross. Now, we have to be careful because excessive guilt means that you're forgetting that Jesus forgave you at the cross. But guilt that simply serves as a reminder of our own sin is a healthy thing.

I grieve for the nonbeliever. He's got to have feelings of guilt. If believers have them, and I've certainly had plenty of them, nonbelievers have them. You can't kill your conscience. This is what the apostle Paul talked about in Romans 2; our consciences are alternately convicting and defending us. What does *conscience* mean other than "with knowledge," if you take the literal construction of the word?

What this means is that every one of us has within us a knowledge of right and wrong, and we know when we've offended this. We know when we've done a wrong thing. I can remember so vividly some of the things I have done in my life that I grieve over because I know I've hurt other people—and I'm being reminded of this now especially with Jonathan Aitken's biography of me. I'm constantly remembering my own sin. That's why I cringe when I receive compliments. I literally do. I know that sounds like self-righteous humility, but it's true—I literally cringe because I really know what I'm capable of. If somebody wants to praise Jesus, that's fine, but praising me is misplaced praise.

Apart from Christ, I'm capable of anything. I can take my sins and my guilt to the cross, but where does the nonbeliever go? How does he deal with the guilt that is inevitable in every life?

Christians have a place where we can go to dump the garbage of our lives, and ironically, we dump it at the cross that stood by Jerusalem's garbage dump; the unbeliever does not.

Sorrow over sin keeps one humble and dependent on God. I don't mean it drives us to the cross in an effort to be saved again; we've been saved once, but as we are reminded of who we are at the feet of Christ, we can never again be arrogant or haughty or proud, because we know the sin we are capable of. It's horrible. And if we know the bad things we've done in our life, the ways in which we've hurt people, then we're equally capable of any sin on par with the most dreadful people in history.

Everyone, believer and nonbeliever alike, comes to the end of himself. But when the believer comes to the end of himself, he merely turns to Christ. For the nonbeliever, the end of life is like stepping off a cliff.

# Facing Reality

I just read a quite interesting article in the *New York Times* Sunday magazine.[2] What it told me, in short, is that there is a continuing hunger for meaning, significance, and what is mistakenly called happiness.

Postmodern people define happiness as hedonism. But of course, it isn't. True happiness is what the Greeks called *eudemonia*, or virtue. It's living a good life. But people also, deep down, have a hunger for transcendence. They want to know God. That's the only way they are going to ultimately find peace. Christians know the *imago Dei* is wired into us.

In today's culture, however, it's not acceptable any longer, when someone is unhappy, to say, well, let's talk to a priest or minister. Today what you do is go to a class on positive psychology—which George Mason University calls the Science of Well-Being—you do your Oprah routine and your yoga, and you listen to some well-meaning psychologists on CDs.

To me, they sound wacko. This is really being carried as a serious discipline in a lot of colleges. Even Harvard is involved in this. It is, as somebody said, almost cultish. It reminds me of what Chesterton said—that when people stop believing in God, they won't believe in nothing, they'll believe in everything. The latest fad to come along, people grab hold of it. It'll die out, like all of these new things, like "I'm Okay, You're Okay," EST, Dale Carnegie techniques, diets. The fads come and go. The interesting thing about the Bible, as I've just written in a book, is that not one word is different today from what it was when the canonical councils finished their work. This is what is so breathtakingly exciting about orthodoxy. It is the pure faith, unaffected over the years by passing fads. But here's the latest fad. It's quite a commentary on human nature and quite a commentary on our culture's unwillingness to face reality and desire to give people euphemisms in the place of the real thing. We're giving them happy pills when they need much sterner stuff.

A couple of months after reading the *New York Times* piece I visited Emily and Max. I was in Boston for a Gordon-Conwell board meeting, so I was able to go down Sunday afternoon and watch Max play basketball in a special needs school. A friend who is not a believer drove me. It was a really interesting experience because I had just been lecturing to the Centurions about the self-absorbed nature of American culture—the fact that people care only about themselves and look out for number one. It is what Robert Bellah calls the age of ontological individualism.[3] The individual is supreme, and most of what we're saying to the government is *keep things off my back; let me do what I want to do*, which is a skewed definition of liberty.

Emily told us that the basketball game was played in an elementary school gymnasium, which is on a lovely, wooded side road in Duxbury. It's an old school. Most of the buildings look like they were built in the thirties; they have that quaint, old New England look, except for the gymnasium, which was recently added on. From the outside it was one of the dreariest-looking buildings I have ever seen. You felt depressed going into the place. Emily commented on it; so did my friend.

But inside, on the basketball court, was one of the most inspiring sights I have ever seen. Here was an assorted group of young people with autism, Down syndrome, and various other disabilities—and they were all out trying to dribble or throw the ball. It was fairly well-organized confusion. There were enough young high-school-aged volunteers that just about every kid had somebody watching out for him. There was a coach there and a couple of other adults who were also helping. Not one kid out of perhaps thirty on the floor could manage for himself.

One of the boys looked to be in his mid-twenties and was helped onto the court by his mother, a woman who just exuded grace. She had that craggy New England look, but a warm, warm smile. And she, as a matter of fact, was smiling most of the time, even as she had to physically hold her son up by the back of the neck. She would take his jacket and literally help him stand. He couldn't speak. He communicated with his eyes, and he seemed very knowing and loving.

What his mother did was take him into the circle where you shoot baskets. One of the volunteers would come over and get his hands onto the ball, and then she would make a great sweeping gesture, and actually *she* would lift the ball out of his hands up into the hoop. This young man got so excited when he saw the ball go into the air and swish through the hoop. He was just beaming, as was his mother.

Max was one of the more functional kids, though he was shooting wild baskets. But the way they run the program is they have a warm-up half hour during which every kid gets to shoot until he sinks a basket. Some of the kids got it on the first throw.

Most of them took two, five or six, or even eight or ten throws. But they all scored a basket. And every time they did, there was this look of joy on their face, on the volunteers' faces, on the family's. There was tremendous excitement.

Then they had a game—half the kids on one team and half on the other. And they ran down the court, bouncing the ball or throwing it back and forth, very clumsily. When they got down to the end, there was no blocking or trying to interfere with the person with the ball. The kid threw it, and then they all jumped for it, and then somebody else threw it. It was all very civilized, all very well organized, and all extremely exciting to these kids.

There was another boy who was autistic, like Max. He moved in almost mechanical, jerky motions, but he had mastered the throw. He threw underhand and hit the basket every time. He would get really excited.

I leaned over to my nonbelieving friend and said, "Watching this makes it kind of hard to believe in Darwin's *Origin of the Species*, doesn't it? The idea that the strong will wipe out the weak, and the survival of the fittest, is the precise opposite of what we are witnessing on this court."

My friend looked at me with the strangest expression. I think he was going to reply, and then decided just not to say anything, because there wasn't anything he could say. It was the most effective refutation of the evolutionary theory I have ever seen in my life.

And it was something else, as well. It was a total antidote to the self-gratification, instant-fix, it's-all-about-me society in which we live. All of these parents devote their lives, as Emily does, to taking care of the kids. That's all they do. The young man I first described who couldn't throw a basketball or talk left his bag on the floor after he and his mother had left. Emily took it back to his mother. It had nothing but diapers in it. Here was a young man in his mid-twenties who was still using diapers, and his mother was so supportive.

But here's the real kick. In this age, where everybody is looking out for themselves, these were among the happiest people I've ever seen. We went into this dreary, drab building, which couldn't have been less inviting. And it was like a celebration. It was like a party inside. It was as thrilling and inspiring as anything I've ever seen.

The lesson is, we are by nature concerned with one another. We do care for each other. It is our natural instinct. Not all of these people were believers. They weren't Christians who were doing it because that's what we Christians are supposed to do; they were doing it because they were human and these kids were their own flesh and blood. But they were getting joy out of it. These people do nothing but give of themselves, and they are the happiest people I've ever seen.

We read about the number of people who are neurotic or depressed in American society and the number of people who suffer from clinical depression. It's because they're trying to do everything for themselves and they can't get all their fun in fast enough. But the people I saw at that gym who do nothing but give of themselves are the happiest people I've ever seen.

As I watched, I thought, *I don't think I could do this. I really doubt that I could trade places with those people. I just don't think I have the patience.* Maybe this is common grace, but I think God gives us a special anointing when we start helping other people. I think that applies to nonbelievers as well as believers.

No one, anyplace, ever, will convince me that Darwin was right when I see the kinds of things I saw in this drab old sandy-colored building on that Sunday afternoon. The answer to evolution takes place there on Sundays when the special needs kids come in.

The irony of that afternoon spent with Max and his friends was not only that it put the lie to Darwin, but ironically, it showed that when we help the sick and suffering instead of doing away with them, we end up surviving better ourselves.

# 7

# HOMOSEXUALITY
## and the CHURCH

# Created for Different Purposes

*In Colorado, the state's Civil Rights Commission ordered Masterpiece Cakeshop owner Jack Phillips to bake wedding cakes for ceremonies of same-sex couples, claiming that the Commission's ruling trumped Phillips's constitutional right to religious freedom and free speech. Church groups have been sued for refusing to rent out their property for homosexual "weddings"; other Christians have sacrificed income for the use of their properties rather than be told by the government that they must rent their property for purposes they find immoral.*

*What would Chuck say to all this? He would urge us to stand firm against the attacks, to speak the truth in love, to offer help to one another, and to support the work of religious legal defense firms such as the Beckett Fund, which take on the attacks on freedom of speech and freedom of religion. If one of your neighbors is fired for refusing to toe the gay line, do what you can to help him. Above all, seek God's wisdom and rely on Him to guide us through these crises.*

*As Chuck's great friend, Professor Robert George of Princeton University, recently put it, we have come to the end of socially acceptable Christianity in America.[1] And, as Chuck notes in this memo, we must teach our children the truth about same-sex attraction and the meaning of marriage — truths they may not hear in school. Finally, we must pray for those caught in the homosexual lifestyle and for those who want to undermine God's plan for human sexuality.*

I've just looked over the CNN transcript of Larry King's interview with Rick Warren talking about homosexuality. It's absolutely marvelous. Warren says that we should explain to seven, eight, or nine-year-old kids that there's a biological difference between men and women, and that they are created for a different purpose, and that this is self-evident when you look at them.

Consider the fact that every civilized society has always honored marriage between a man and a woman. In ancient times, and even in some cases in modern times, polygamy has been accepted.

As Christians we don't recommend that; it's an exploitation of women. Jesus Himself defines marriage as a union of one man and one woman (Mark 10:6–7). And Paul orders church leaders to have just one wife (1 Timothy 3:2, 12).

We do not live in a perfect world; things do go wrong. Mothers die, or fathers die. Parents remarry, and children are raised partly by stepparents. In some cases, though it's not a good thing, two men will act as mommy and daddy, or two women will.

But we know that there is a special role that a mother plays with a child, and a special role that a father plays. They're complementary. Kids need both. Boys especially need a male role model, and that's what the dad is. They need to be responsible teachers of their kids, and play sports with their boys — the things boys do. Unfortunately, where that doesn't happen, boys will look for male role models elsewhere.

We need to teach our kids that there is such a thing as moral truth. Even when they are just six or seven, children can know that the word *truth* means the way things really are; that is, what conforms to reality. Obviously, you put this in kid language. But give them illustrations. For instance, you could use the law of gravity. And then explain that we have the same kind of laws regarding how we behave with one another.

I think the thing you want to get across is that the world is made a certain way, and figuring out how it works is the biggest challenge in life. And then just explain to them the most fundamental truth: that we were created in the image of God; that we fell into sin by rebellion against God, but that God has saved us through Christ; and that we have to live our lives for Him. The Bible guides us on how we should live, and the evidence teaches us that the Bible's teachings on how we should live work better than anything else.

When people stay within a marriage there is less disease and illness; there's a better climate for kids. We all know this; the evidence is overwhelming. That tells us that this is the true way to live.

You can make your arguments more sophisticated as your children get older. It's been a long time since I taught my kids anything, but I can't believe that this couldn't be communicated in a simple, understandable way to children. I think you have to underscore in this whole presentation that there are a lot of people who don't live this way, and we think they are making a mistake. But we should not be unkind to them; we should not call them names; we should not be judgmental. We know that we don't want to live that way, but we should love them anyway.

# Our Highest Priority

I have just read a memo with talking points on the Marriage Amendment and why homosexual "marriage" would undermine genuine marriage. There are one or two good points, but by and large, it is mush. If I were reading this and knew nothing about the issues, I would wonder what possible harm could be done by allowing homosexuals to "marry." There's not a single good argument made that we are undermining the exclusive and preferred role of marriage in society, a status given because of its public policy importance.

There is a wonderful prudential case to be made on the natural order here. Princeton professor Robert George has done it.[2] Jennifer Roback Morse has as well.[3] So has Jay Budziszewski.[4]

I consider it a matter of absolute highest priority that Christian leaders get some good natural-order talking points down on paper regarding marriage. We've given special rights and privileges to the institution of marriage throughout recorded history to protect the family, both for procreation and for rearing children, as well as for domestic stability. We have to show why we're not dealing with civil rights here with homosexual sex. If people want to engage in it in the privacy of their homes, it's clear that states cannot prevent it; that's okay. But you can't go the next step and say that homosexual relationships should be given the same legal status as heterosexual marriage without weakening the preferred status heterosexual marriage has always had for good, prudential reasons.

# In His Image

In the last few weeks I've been talking quite a bit about same-sex "marriage" on *BreakPoint*. I don't know what kind of response those commentaries are getting, but I've been sensing a real deadening of interest in the Christian world. I think people have resigned themselves to the fact that we're going to have gay "marriage" and that's the way it's going to be. So that sense of outrage and shock has worn off—which is the way all liberal movements work. They grind us down. I'd like to do a *BreakPoint* broadcast in which I speak directly to individual listeners and say, first of all, that it's just sinful when we throw up our hands and say there's nothing we can do. The gay rights juggernaut is grinding down on us. It's the most ominous threat on the horizon in America, and with all the threats we have that's a pretty big statement—because it threatens not only to institute something that is an abomination to God, but also to crush our religious liberties in the process.

The whole plan of creation is embodied in the first three chapters of Genesis, particularly the end of chapter 2 through parts of chapter 3, where we get the macro picture of human relationships, what it means to be made in the image of God, and how and why God created us and for what purpose. You will see there that He created man; He then created woman out of man's rib. And what's the next thing He did? He joined man and woman together as one flesh. And we learn that procreation, the perpetuation of the human race, is one of His purposes for humanity.

The critical thing here is that this applies to everybody, not just Christians, because it is pre-fall. In other words, if you believe that God has created us in His image (which I'll bet you 80 percent of Americans do), then you have to say that He made us as man and woman. And He immediately joined the first humans as one flesh.

Marriage isn't just an agreement; marriage isn't just a thing where we all pick a mate and that's it. Marriage is part of the creation plan. It is pre-fall, and it applies to all human beings. When people deconstruct marriage and make it two men or two women, who cannot become one flesh, we are upsetting the original plan of creation.

That's why this issue is so critical. Homosexual "marriage" is redefining who we are. It's redefining what the creation is about and what it's for. It isn't simply about any two (or more) people of the same sex coming together, enjoying each other, and sharing joint benefits.

This is why the church has traditionally called marriage a sac-rament—which, of course, it has to be, even though we don't call it that in many churches today, sad to say. We call marriage a sac-rament because it is a sign of God and His creation. It's the defini-tion of the word *creation*. We've got to restore this and teach it in the churches. We've got to take this simple little nugget of truth and build on it so that eventually we permeate public conscious-ness with the realization that this isn't just about equality. This isn't just about rights for gays versus straights. This isn't about civil rights. This is about the plan of creation. And if we destroy that, we're going to bring the wrath of God upon us. We're actu-ally going to destroy the very nature of the world we live in, the very purpose of the world and the very purpose of life.

# A New Dark Ages

I believe we are headed for a new Dark Ages, with persecution coming to the church soon. It's going to happen as a result of conflicts over sex. This is where modern human beings do not want to be in any way restrained. They will accept the law that governs them in just about every area of their lives except sexual passions.

The entire sixties movement for personal autonomy was over sex. Phillip Johnson argues that the entire culture war is rooted in sex, and that the destruction of the rule of law itself is traceable to the desire for total sexual freedom. Freudianism, he says, has taken a much deeper hold than we realize.[5]

If you look at all the major Supreme Court cases, you will see that they all deal with sexual rights, from *Roe v. Wade* to *Casey v. Planned Parenthood* to the *Romer* and *Lawrence* decisions. The desire to give sexual license to people, and remove all restraints, has resulted in our losing restraints in many other areas. In other words, it's libertinism run amok.

How strongly does this affect our religious liberties? Well, are we going to be required to perform gay "marriages" when the court rules that marriage is an inherent civil right? If pastors are willing to marry heterosexual couples, how can they then refuse to "marry" gay couples? Critics will ask, isn't this just like the racial divide issues and misogyny statues?

Preaching against homosexuality is already a crime in Canada and Denmark. Here in America, we have a series of hate crime bills that are beginning to develop a body of law that holds homosexual "marriage" to be a civil right on a par with heterosexual marriages, meaning one may not discriminate against homosexual couples. The next step will be requiring churches to perform these "marriage" services.

We're already in the position of being denied federal funds if we won't hire homosexuals. Remember, they said this would be decided on a case-by-case basis, but you know exactly where this is heading.[6]

The place I expect to see the break in the wall is the tax exemption. I think Christian tax-exempt charities and even churches are in peril because we will not be allowed to "discriminate" against homosexuals any more than we would be allowed to engage in racial discrimination. The logic tells me this is coming.

So what do Christians do? We fight every inch of the way. But we must also prepare ourselves by discipling people to be courageous about proclaiming their faith. And if we lose our tax exemption, we find ways to make greater use of volunteers and get used to going lean. We're certainly not going to conform — Lord help us! The German Church gave in during the thirties, which gave Hitler the power he needed; the Barmen Declaration came too late to stop him. So the church will have to hold its ground and refuse to knuckle under. It's going to take a lot of creative thinking, and it's going to be one whale of a fight.

We must also reflect on how we defend religious liberty. We don't want to defend it by claiming our opponents are bigots. Instead, we have to show why, if we allow the government to take away freedom of conscience, we're going to lose all other liberties. That's the kind of approach that is going to have to be made to get a majority of the people with us. It might not help in the courts, but at least we can begin to win some public support.

# Hearts and Minds

The battle to stop homosexual "marriage" is going to be waged in legislatures across the country. But an even more important battle is going to be waged for the hearts and minds of citizens, because the court is going to listen to the cultural consensus. So it is absolutely vital, urgent, that Christians begin to make an apologetic defense of why marriage should be limited to male and female couples — that is, natural marriage.

We also need to learn what *not* to do. Just look at the debate that took place in the House of Representatives over the Defense of Marriage Act. Some congressmen stood up and read the Bible; others talked about what an abominable sin homosexual behavior is in God's eyes, which led to all the liberals charging that this was an attempt by the religious right to exploit prejudices against gays. It was gay bashing; it was homophobic; it was singling out one group for discrimination. Why in the world should we not allow gay couples to get "married," if they want to? The only people against it are those repressive Christians quoting their Bibles.

Even though we won the vote in Congress, we ultimately lost in the court of public opinion. We're painted as bigots in the media; we're driven into the corner. And the Supreme Court, which will ultimately have the final say and has already tipped its hand in *Romer*, will rule against us.

So how do we argue? First of all, we have to argue that there are certain normative standards that a society must follow, and it's not wrong to set normative standards. We say, for example, that someone shouldn't carry a concealed weapon, or we say that people shouldn't vote until they are eighteen. Society does set certain rules for civilized behavior, and one of those rules is that marriage is between a man and a woman. The moment that we say that marriage can take place between any two people we are taking away its distinctiveness. Representative Barney Frank's big argument was that if two loving males want to live together as a "married" couple, why should we think that their doing so undermines marriage? It does so because it takes away what society has labeled as normative and makes homosexual "marriage" the moral equivalent of heterosexual marriage.

And it can't be the moral equivalent because it can't constitute the same role model that every society throughout history has established of a man and a woman raising children. It can't provide for procreation except through the petri dish.

But in today's libertinism run amok, people—particularly judges—are going to be very, very moved by Barney Frank's basic argument. Why not?

So the first argument that has to be dealt with is why it is wrong to say that they are morally equivalent. They are not morally equivalent. There is a fundamental difference, and society has the right to choose in favor of normative, genuine marriage over "marriage" between any two people who happen to be fond of each other.

We then move into the point that this is a cultural battle, and we've got to make an argument, an apologetic, something that gets our points across to people in an easily understood way. To say, "the Bible says" is probably counterproductive because we then fall into the trap of being looked upon as Bible-pounding bigots on the right who are trying to impose their morality on others. Instead, we should be arguing for what is good and prudential and just and right for society.

I like the arguments made by David Coolidge—that there is a natural law, there is a moral law just as there are physical laws. And societies throughout history have recognized these.

# First Things

*On a* BreakPoint *broadcast, Chuck noted, "Freedom of religion means you can practice your faith in public, you can educate your children in the faith, you can evangelize.... Freedom of worship, however, is something less. It means you can worship how you please, so long as you keep it private. Citizens of the former Soviet Union could do that. And China has that law today."*

I was dismayed when Hillary Clinton made her speech at Georgetown University [in 2009], in which she said there were three great human rights that she would stand for. One was the right to form your own government, the second was the right to love anyone else in any way you chose, and the third one was the "right to worship."[7]

I was distressed first that she would reduce "freedom of religion" to "freedom of worship." We know the distinction there, but it's a good time to remind people of that. But I was really shocked that she would put those two on a morally equivalent line. In other words, freedom of sexual expression, to me, is nowhere near the revered right of religious liberty, or freedom of conscience, which is another way to put it.

Among America's founders, there was great discussion about this, on Madison's part in particular, as I recall. And in the great debate over the Bill of Rights it was interesting that the first freedom guaranteed was the right to freedom of religion. Why would conscience be first? Because without freedom of conscience, you don't have any other freedoms. If people tell you what you have to believe and how you have to believe, and they control that, then you're no longer free. One could make a pretty good side observation here that all the pressures in our society—trying to control the language we use, what is politically correct, what isn't—is all limiting free expression of our own conscience—what we believe.

But now, religious freedom may have to settle for equality with freedom of sexual expression, because it is overriding religious freedom at every turn. This is the battle we're having with a number of great cultural pressures. We can't stand for the Defense of

Marriage Act, even if, with us, it's a matter of religious conscience, because to do so is "to do harm to gays." There's also the situation where the law firm King & Spalding withdrew its decision to defend the Defense of Marriage Act after tremendous pressure from homosexual rights groups. So we're really being pushed into a corner by a small but vocal and extraordinarily powerful lobby. It's making sexual expression trump freedom of conscience.

This is the ultimate victory of Freud. Freud was not entirely wrong, because he talked about the hormonal urge being primal and driving things. But unrestrained sexual expression did not bring us liberty, as he thought it would; it brought us repression and slavery. To imagine that we would put sexual expression on an equal par, let alone make it superior to freedom of religious expression and conscience, would cause our founders to come right back from the grave. This is blasphemy against the whole American dream.

It is, of course, totally contrary to a biblical worldview, which reveres freedom of conscience as the obvious first right, because man is made in the image of God, and is free to accept Him or reject Him. Our conscience is to be bound only by what we know to be true and by the Word of God.

But this is our first right, and Christians have always regarded this as paramount. We would surrender a lot to protect the freedom of conscience of a Muslim, for example.

This is an area that is becoming very timely. It would be good to remind people of some basics about what is the first liberty, what is the first right, what are the first things.

# An Absolute Duty

The survival of the human race depends upon marriage as the institution by which we procreate and perpetuate civilization. Your view of marriage depends upon whether you believe we are just two free agents with no moral restraints and desire to make an agreement that we're going to live together in whatever relationship we want to live in, and the state and the church have nothing to say about it. If you're a naturalist, that's quite logical. If you are not a naturalist—if you believe in God—then you believe God ordained this structure, because He said He did. You believe that two people—a man and a woman—have joined together as one flesh in order to procreate.

Matrimony comes from *mater*, meaning mother. So when the word appears in the *Book of Common Prayer* of the seventeenth century, it is talking about two people entering into the state in which children will be produced, which is why it was a sacrament in the church. Historically, marriage still is a sacrament in the Catholic Church, though not in the evangelical church. But marriage should be treated as sacred, as you would treat a sacrament, because it is a sign of our faith. And Christians, when we fight gay "marriage," we're on shaky ground, because it was the dissolution of the sacred understanding of marriage that has opened the door to people saying they simply want to live together. And they have every right to. The California Supreme Court said it was a natural right, meaning people are born with the right to get married, which of course is an oxymoron; it's impossible just by definition.

This is a great issue to talk about, but it's not just about the battles going on in the courts. It's a good chance to do a reality check. We should be teaching about the fundamental presuppositions that inform the decisions we make in public policy. If you make a public policy decision based on an ideology, it's going to be a mistake. Instead, you make a public policy decision based upon worldview. The worldview starts with one question: Did God create, or didn't He?

One of the things that disturbs me most is that I think the ordinary Christian is not prepared to defend the truths of marriage, as basic as they may seem to us. When our elites start talking about polygamy, for instance, I think many Christians do not understand the framework of Scripture to be able to argue these things. It scares me that this is going to continue to become an issue that divides our churches.

We have an absolute duty to start training our children in biblical worldview when they are just beyond the toddler years. They've got to start understanding that there are some basic truths in life, and that if we abandon them, the whole scheme of living unravels. And marriage is a great example, because very, very few evangelicals, at least that I talk to, have ever heard of marriage talked about this way. They see it as a covenant with one another and with God—the more devout see it that way— but very few people see it as part of the structure of life built into the fact that God has created us and given us, in His Word, an understanding of man and woman as one, and why that is so, and the purpose of it.

If we were to educate people about this, there'd be no case for gay "marriage."

But if we teach kids that sexual expression is just a matter of personal preference, that sex doesn't have any moral component, nor does it have any natural or physical order to it, that we are whatever we want to be and we may gratify ourselves any way we feel like it, then it's impossible for marriage to be limited to a man and a woman.

In a very short time it will be impossible to preach that homosexual behavior is a sin. How do you teach that something is a sin when society is saying it is simply a legitimate choice? This is the camel's nose under the tent. This is why the homosexual issue is about a lot more than gay rights. It's about deconstructing the moral order of society, and the people behind it know that. They really are moral nihilists at heart.

# Where Is Our Courage?

I recently had a conversation with a friend who is a member of a very strong evangelical church. He told me he met with his pastor to urge him to get more involved in some of the worldview issues and cultural battles of the day. The pastor drew back in his chair and said, "You know, my friend, I have one great regret about my ministry. It is that I got involved in the debate over gay marriage. Do you realize we lost several members over that?"

My friend was speechless. What do you say to someone who denies the clear teaching of Scripture — or, in this case, stands up for it and then regrets it?

What is grievously missing in today's church is one of the four great virtues. I think the most important one is courage. Can you imagine being afraid of losing a few members when you speak the truth? Can you imagine praying at night that God will lead you in your work, and then denying biblical truth when you're confronted with it in society?

I wish I could say this was an isolated story, but I have heard four or five instances of this same type of thing — in fact, probably more than that. Most of them are secondhand. San Diego pastor Jim Garlow has talked about all the people in California who backed away from supporting Proposition 8 because they couldn't take the pressure. Or look at some of the companies that have caved in to boycott threats from the gay lobby.

Courage, by its very definition, means you overcome a natural fear of doing something. It doesn't mean that you don't fear it. Bravery is not a lack of fear; it is the willingness to do what you have to do, overcoming fear to do so.

A great example of this in modern times is Dietrich Bonhoeffer. He had the courage to defy the Nazis at the cost of his life. He never backed away, never retreated. The story of his actual death, the way he prayed before he was hanged, is unforgettable.

If we believe God's Word is true, if we believe it applies to us, of course we're going to be afraid to take an unpopular stand. When it comes to standing up for biblical marriage nobody likes to be called a bully; nobody likes to be called a bigot; nobody likes to rock the boat. And nobody likes to lose members of their church.

I think the attacks on Christians for their stand on marriage is the latest assault by the left on religious liberty. It's going to be the acid test. Martin Luther King Jr. quoted Augustine, who wrote that an unjust law is no law at all. If we're not willing to fight this, even to the point of breaking the law, or refusing to recognize the law, then we will lose everything. I think our backs are to the wall, and if your pastor doesn't have the courage to speak out on this issue, look for another church.

The virtue of courage is lost. I don't think people understand it, or even think through what it means. And if anybody should have courage, it's not the eighteen-year-old who throws himself into combat. It's the pastor who has a comfortable, established life and has to risk it all to be faithful to the call of God.

# The Drip, Drip, Drip Approach

The way our adversaries work is like this: They say something considered positively outrageous, scandalous, and everybody just recoils in horror. Then you start the discussion. And the other side starts to back off a little bit, and gradually gets away from the original sensational statement. Then they use the drip, drip, drip approach. They keep talking about it, and all of a sudden it begins to sound normal, and then they just keep gradually moving the goalposts. Before you know it, the ideas the other side is pushing have become okay.

Look at the whole gay issue. Not long ago, homosexuality was something that was in the closet — something nobody talked about. I was accused, in the 1972 presidential campaign, of planting homosexuals in George McGovern's office to make him look bad. Frank Mankowicz, who was one of the Democratic gurus of the day, wrote a book about it; it was one of Colson's dirty tricks. I didn't do it. As a matter of fact, I jokingly told the press I didn't have to because there were plenty of them already there.[8]

But in those days it was a stigma. Then you notice how, gradually, piece by piece, they began to make their behavior seem normal. Then you saw courses in universities on gender selection and the idea that gender was a matter of choice, not biology. You began to see gay activists asking for the outrageous: marriage. Then, of course, they retreated and went for civil unions. And eventually, we got civil unions, and civil unions become marriage by another name.

Now look at the debate going on regarding whether homosexual behavior is immoral. What has for centuries been regarded as immoral and a perversion, a distortion of the natural or created order, has now become moral. In fact, it is an act of bigotry to criticize it. This is incrementalism, cushioning us against what seems so hard at first. You just kind of get used to it; it's like pornography. After a while, people don't think it's so bad after all; they just get used to it.

# Warning from Scandinavia

I began to think very differently about the marriage issue because of the arguments of Stanley Kurtz, particularly in an article titled "The End of Marriage in Scandinavia," which reveals a link between acceptance of gay "marriage" and the disintegration of marriage itself, and the negative effect upon children. The article points out that "same-sex marriage has locked in and reinforced an existing Scandinavian trend towards the separation of marriage and parenthood."[9] What came through to me was the realization that separating parenthood from marriage is really at the heart of the problem.

The moment you look at marriage as nothing but a contract between two parties to express their mutual affection, which gays of course can readily subscribe to, and separate it from procreation and the rearing of children, you've lost the battle. You've not only lost the battle, you've lost civilization.

I'm not overdramatizing that. You really have.

What makes life go around is the desire to reproduce yourself and have children and see those children grow up and do better than you did. It's the way in which you seek some connection with the moral order of the universe. In effect, we create a legacy of our lives through our children. Now, if we see that role—that is, children carrying on after us—separate from creating a relationship with another partner, then of course, the whole house of cards collapses. You can have children today without getting married, with little or no social condemnation. Or you can get married and decide against having children.

You could compartmentalize your life. You could say, "Who is it that I want to get into an intimate partnership with to enjoy the sexual experience?" People make one decision about with whom to share their lives, and then make another decision about having children. It may be that the person they decide to share their life with will also be their children's biological mother or father. But not necessarily.

Once you establish this kind of thinking, which is what has happened in Scandinavia, there's no incentive to marry. Why get married?

The problem is, of course, that every society has eventually discovered what the Bible teaches, and that is that the family is the bedrock institution of society. It's what keeps everything from spinning out of control.

What I've been thinking about is an absolute nightmare scenario—the triumph of Rousseau, where we just couple with anybody we want to couple with, for whatever period of time we feel like we want to do it, no real commitment there. And then we go about acquiring kids—however we decide to acquire them, or in whatever way is most convenient for us.

The utopian scheme that people honestly think is going to work better, won't. This is a dangerous, dangerous agenda.

# The Wedge Issue

I just read an incredible piece by Laurie Goodstein on page one of the *New York Times*. On Christmas Day! Only the

*Times* would do this. The headline read, "At Axis of the Episcopal Split, an Anti-gay Nigerian."[10] The article, as you can probably surmise, was an attack on the bishop that many of the American Anglican churches were affiliating with: Bishop Peter Akinola. He was against ordaining gays in the church, as I am, and everyone else is. According to the article, he is in favor of a bill in the Nigerian legislature that would make homosexual sex and any public expression of it a crime. That I certainly don't favor, and I wonder if that is really true.

The press is going after Episcopal churches that are spinning off over the issue of orthodoxy and belief in the Bible.[11]

The issue is not homosexuality. Homosexual behavior is merely a sign of the rebellion of those who choose to disbelieve the Bible. But had they grounded this assault on any other grounds, like the historicity of the resurrection, you would see the same things happen. All of this press reaction is intended, particularly so in the *Times*, to make us look bigoted.

I know that we are supposed to overcome evil with good, but I think we are also on occasion supposed to straighten out people when they are this far wrong. I take a lot of offense with the particular charge that we are anti-gay, since I can remember when I visited a prison inmate named Bessie Ship, who was dying of AIDS. At that time, nobody knew how you got AIDS and I was holding Bessie's hand, leading her to Christ in a death row cell in prison. I have since then ministered to I can't tell you how many hundreds of men with AIDS. I have never shied away from them. I have prayed with them, I love them, and I am not against them.

But I am against a practice that is picked out in Romans 1 as the ultimate rebellion against the natural order. Romans 1 talks about the natural order being visible, that which is made plain to people. It then immediately says that those who deny this have exchanged the truth for a lie. It then goes on to talk about homosexual relations. Most people don't see the connection, but there is a connection. Paul is saying that there is a physical created order that everybody can see. It is in nature, witnessing to the reality of God.

The Book of Nature does not end with physical nature; it goes to the moral nature, as well.[12] Because the moral nature is that behavior that conforms to the physical order. Homosexual sin is no greater a sin than heterosexual sin. It is just that it is more of an explicit rejection of the created moral and physical order, because men and women are designed differently.

If the church denies any one of the fundamentals of the faith — and one of the fundamentals has to be that God has spoken and His Word is clear and we accept it as His Word — then a church split is going to result. It has already been going on quite a while over this issue. So why was it front page news? Because the *Times* wanted to make us look bigoted.

This issue is not going to go away because people are going to keep hitting us over the head until they deny us the right to be able to speak about what is biblical sin. The homosexual issue is the wedge issue that the other side is using. Therefore, it is absolutely imperative that Christians figure out how to answer this and not let this whole bigotry steamroller crush us. Regarding Anglicans — they are not breaking up the church over beliefs and teachings about homosexual activity; they are breaking up the church over fidelity to the Bible. And that is what really needs to be stressed and understood.

# The Ultimate Absurdity

The state of California has now granted conjugal visiting rights to homosexual inmates. When we talked about all the problems related to recognizing civil unions, everybody said it was hysteria, that there would be no problems, and that they ought to be treated like everyone else.

Well, here is the ultimate absurdity — well, maybe not the ultimate, but close to it. The biggest problem in prisons is homosexual sex, particularly predatory sex. Most of the fights, most of the stabbings, most of the really dangerous situations arise over the tensions that come from homosexuality. That's an unnatural environment, where there is no heterosexual sex inside the prison unless it is between female inmates and male guards. Homosexual sex is rampant.

Now the state wants to recognize the right for conjugal visits. Prisoners don't need it. They already have homosexual sex in the prison. What the state is doing is normalizing it. What they are saying is that gay sex is okay with a chosen partner who happens to have certain legal rights granted by the state, which will be recognized on a weekend visit. But inside the prison, sex between prisoners is a cause for disciplinary action, because it will lead to riots. Talk about making normal a practice that is demonstratively dangerous inside the prison.

This is where all of this nonsense, this unraveling of the classical social contract, is going to leave us: in complete bedlam.

This is a policy that will be deeply resented by heterosexual inmates who don't get a chance to see their partners very often, and by the homosexual inmates who will say certain homosexuals are getting particularly favored treatment. If you start messing with this kind of arrangement, you will have real troubles.

# 8

# ISLAM VERSUS CHRISTIANITY

# The Irrepressible
# Desire for Freedom

Anytime there's a crisis in the Middle East, the Christian's first thought is "end times." Tumultuous events raise the specter of the return of Christ, the fulfillment of biblical prophecy.

None of us know the time and place of Christ's return—something Christ Himself reminded us of. Instead, the most urgent question posed by Middle East blow-ups should be: What are the worldview implications of this?

When people write to me about the Middle East, their first concern is whether this will fuel what Samuel Huntington prophesied as the clash of civilizations. Huntington, in his 1998 book by that title, predicted that the titanic struggle of the twenty-first century would be fought between Islam and Western culture formed by Judeo-Christian tradition.[1]

Christians should understand the fundamental differences between Islam and Christianity. We can't be very good advocates of our own belief system if we can't draw that comparison in a very honest and sincere way. We are also obligated to distinguish radical Islam—that is, the jihadist movement—from peace-loving Muslims. This is not only a matter of being fair and objective in our evaluation; it's also a matter of not fanning the flames of what could turn into a worldwide conflagration.

The best estimate I've heard of the number of British Muslims who are in sympathy with the jihadist movement is 20 percent.[2] That's a formidable bloc. The West cannot deal with this crisis if we do not understand the dynamics of the Muslim world and particularly the jihadist wing of Islam. The idea that we can fight terrorism without understanding who perpetrates terror and why they do it is dangerously delusional.

The second issue has to do with the dignity of human life. Christians believe that all humans, not just Christians and Jews, are created in the image of God. Every human, therefore, has innate dignity. Many people believe that this can be known by human reason, and in one sense they are correct. It is self-evident that we are different from all other creatures.

Third, what we are witnessing in the Middle East today is the irrepressible desire for freedom that is wired into every human being. The biblical worldview is the only worldview that recognizes this, which clearly sets forth humanity as created in the image of God with innate dignity. The words of the Declaration of Independence capture this beautifully.

In cultures that are informed by Judeo-Christian truth, therefore, there is a built-in respect for human beings and human freedom. We do see this as a self-evident truth; no other worldview sees human beings this way. No other worldview forms its governing structures in a way to cause freedom to flourish. This is one of the things that distinguish a culture informed by Christian revelation from one that is not. Remember, democracy began as a concept in the monasteries, and took root in the governing structures during the Reformation.

A very cogent argument can be made that only the Christian worldview provides for governing structures that take into account the right balance between the goodness of human beings and our fallen nature; that the Christian worldview best accommodates humanity's innate desire for freedom, but balances it with the necessary order so that freedom does not become license. Christians have a very, very appealing worldview to those who are willing to think through these kinds of questions.

# The Clash of Civilizations

I read an extraordinary article by Thomas Friedman that illustrates why, in the clash of civilizations, the West has flourished and Islam has failed: Islam does not have a concept of forgiveness and reconciliation.[3] The article featured an Arab leader, a Syrian-born poet, who critiques Islam and points out that the lack of forgiveness and ability to reconcile, as well as a lack of creative capacity, dooms them, whereas this is precisely the secret of the success of the West.

Here is your clash of worldviews. And by the way, here also is the ultimate answer to the clash of civilizations. We Christians need to advance this concept of reconciliation and how it is possible. It seems to me that Friedman, who's brilliant and one of the few columnists in the *Times* I sometimes agree with, has put his finger on the issue here. Actually, if you read the whole piece, you'll see the Qur'an talks about Mohammed as a prophet of mercy. Then he goes on to say these peace-loving ideas — that is, reconciliation and forgiveness — are lost in the Muslim world today, maybe because of their hatred of us. But they're only destroying themselves.

This is where the Christian message can really resonate with Muslims. They need to see how this works in the West and understand this. What a great message this would be to get to the Islamic world. And what a great testimony it is regarding the truth and viability of the biblical worldview.

It's amazing to hear a Muslim recognizing the superiority of the Christian worldview. Because Islam has no sense of forgiveness and reconciliation, there's no sense of grace. So they get themselves in a box where there's all this hatred between the different Islamic strains, and they have no way to pull it together; they're killing each other and us in the process.

# Islam Behind Bars

I just read a *Wall Street Journal* article about Muslim influence in prisons. Nothing in this article surprised me. It described what I expected was happening — but of course we previously had no direct evidence. If you've spent any time in a prison, you've sensed the kind of environment in which radical Islam can flourish. If you've spent as much time talking to inmates over the years as I have, you know that there is that seed of anger and resentment that would take very little to exploit.

I think we need to give very careful thought to where we should deal with this issue—and if so, how. It is clearly a world-view/comparative religion argument; it's an issue that's important for Christians to understand. One's first reaction is that we should discuss it and attempt to educate people. I think it is a very serious problem and prisons could well be a principal breeding ground for terrorism.

My initial response is tempered by three things. First, we don't want to be saying things that will in any way hamper ministry efforts to work in the prisons. A piece I wrote got some adverse reaction from liberal chaplains, which was understandable, but I don't want to create a backlash that makes it harder for us to minister.

Secondly, I really do recognize what Bush and others are try-ing to do, which is to avoid a confrontation with Islam. So I think it's incumbent on religious leaders to not make inflammatory statements. We need to be honest and forthright about our beliefs, but this is not a time to ignite passions.

My third reaction is that anything that interferes with the right of Muslims to practice their faith in the prisons is going to work to our disadvantage. Even apart from any selfish interest in this, we are committed to pluralism and religious freedom. There is a sharp division within Christian ranks on the roots of religious freedom and how it's interpreted. Seamus Hasson of the Becket Fund for Religious Liberty takes an anthropological position; that is, every human being is entitled to have his or her religious rights protected, which is why the Becket Fund will defend Muslims as quickly as they'll defend Christians.

Other Christian groups believe that Christians are only required to protect the religious rights of Christians and we shouldn't have anything to do with defending the religious rights of others.

I fall into the first camp. Our national creed, which to me is the opening of the Declaration of Independence, makes it very clear that *all* men are created equal. So I'm willing to defend the rights of other people's beliefs, even when I think they're fundamentally wrong. This, to me, is the very heart of the definition of tolerance in American life.

Having said all that, I feel very strongly that you would not allow a religious sect of any kind to preach, especially in a prison, a doctrine that promotes violence. If the *Wall Street Journal* article is to be believed, and I think it is, that's precisely what is happening. That's wrong. That's a perversion of religious liberty, which, if not checked, undermines everyone's religious liberty.

This issue has come up with respect to the Aryan Brotherhood, which I suppose has some parallels with extreme Islam. These people claim to be Christians, but they want to "purify" the race. They're locked up in the prisons; they're segregated. They don't have Aryan Brotherhood preachers coming in and talking to them. There's a parallel here in my mind.

But a second issue is raised by the aggressiveness with which the Saudis are training people in sending materials into the US that end up in our prisons. Wahhabism is an extreme form of Islam, and Saudi Arabia is actively trying to spread their doctrine in our prisons. If we are applying an analogy of free trade, we allow other countries' imports into our country that won't allow our exports into theirs. Can you imagine what would happen if we sent Bibles to a group in Saudi Arabia to distribute in the Saudi prisons? Whoever did this would be beheaded. American personnel in Saudi Arabia can't even practice their faith in their homes. That's the difference between a free society and a theocracy.

To me this is a legitimate issue that must be addressed. If the Saudis are deliberately trying to plant Wahhabism in the prisons, that's not a religious liberty question; that's like us trying to plant not just Christianity, but Aryan Christianity in the Saudi prisons. I don't think when Jefferson wrote the words of our national creed he ever intended that we would take a benign attitude toward any kind of so-called religious influence coming into our prisons. I don't think he was thinking, either, of the differences between a free pluralistic society and a theocracy.

The problem here is that at root Islam is a theocracy, so they basically have to penetrate our country and build a revolution. It's illogical to think that they would want to do anything else. This is clearly what Islam is about. This is not ranting on our part, this is fact. The only issue is whether Islamists carry out their beliefs. If they want to deny their own beliefs, then they're benign; but if they exercise them, they're not.

The really fundamental question is: What does a pluralistic free society, which respects the rights of all people to practice their faith, do with a theocratic and sometimes violent religion?

If we're in the business of promoting a biblical worldview, it's almost impossible to ignore this question. We are experiencing a clash of civilizations whether anybody likes it or not.

# Undermining Radical Islam

*Chuck was deeply involved in the Centurions program and enjoyed responding to letters participants sent to him on various subjects.*

Thanks very much for raising the questions about *The Clash of Civilizations* and the position taken by Professor Moshe Sharon of Hebrew University of Jerusalem. I haven't had a chance to download it yet and read it, but I think I know his thesis. He takes a very hardline Zionist position and makes a case that on its face is logically pretty hard to assail.

Islam, if you read it literally and take it seriously, cannot rest until it has erased Jews, Christians, infidels, and all others who stand in the way of the fulfillment of Islam, that is, worldwide Islam. It is a theocratic religion that advances by force. That's why it is so deadly dangerous, why you've heard me say many times that we are in a real serious war that will last for a long time, probably a couple of generations.

If I wanted to be a pessimist I would agree with Professor Sharon. On the logic of the matter there can never be any détente with Islam. But all human problems aren't settled logically.

My belief is that President George W. Bush's strategy is to plant democracy in the Middle East. Yes, he's having a very tough time of it in Iraq, and yes, a betting man would probably not bet he would succeed. But I'm hoping and praying he does succeed because there is no other long-term solution other than our being at continuous loggerheads with much of the Muslim world.

The strategy is that no matter how intractable hardline Islamic teachings are, democracy planted in the Middle East would prove so attractive to the masses of people who have been impoverished and basically enslaved by ruthless Muslim leaders that the pressure would build to overthrow repressive regimes. The theory is, as well, that moderate Muslim regimes would begin to embrace democracy as, of course, Turkey has.

We are not going to win in a toe-to-toe, head-to-head confrontation with radical Islam. All you can do is undermine it from within. In other words, offer an alternative that is so attractive that the masses of Muslims begin to demand it and moderate governments begin to embrace it. It's going to be a long bloody clash, however. As Samuel Huntington said, "Islam has bloody borders,"[4] and indeed it does.

Bush's strategy, if I'm right about it, is a very biblical one; it is overcoming evil with good. It is going into the Middle East and establishing a beachhead for democracy on the premise that the people of that region will then want it and demand it. Who knows whether we can succeed, but I can't think of anything else we can do other than try. This is why, even though we didn't find weapons of mass destruction, I think it was right for us to go into Iraq. All of us should be praying that it succeeds.

Remember that this very strategy did succeed with the Soviet Union and Communism. So be an optimist.

# Overcoming Evil with Good

Some say the issue of the Old Testament and the fact that God wiped out the Canaanites, for example, is analogous to what Islam is doing today.[5] Not so. First of all, we see in the Old Testament warring tribes were under no authority structure. The covenant people were battling for land that God had given them against others who did not know our God. So one can understand in ancient times that these kinds of wars would result.

As for the destruction of the Canaanites, for example, I believe it is an historical fact, but we find it in Scripture mainly because of its metaphorical value. What God is attempting to show to the Israelites is that He wants them to be pure and holy. He therefore does not want them mixing with the unholy. I always looked upon the killing of the Canaanites as an act of purging in which God is proving He will accept nothing less than holiness.

Harsh? Yes, of course, the Old Testament is filled with very harsh judgment and teachings. However, that is why the new covenant is so dramatically different. God is no longer wiping people out for their unholiness or punishing them in that way for their sin. He sends His Son to die on the cross for all of our sins; for all who will believe, which could embrace Muslims, Buddhists, Hindus, and any other group. This is the extraordinary part of the New Testament and of the gospel message. This is love incarnate. This is a concern for every human being.

I believe the Bible to be true, but my intimate knowledge of God is through the New Testament. The Jew might have a tough time in his argument with Islam. And he certainly does, as you can see violence like that in the Old Testament taking place in Israel and Palestine today. But the Christian never has to apologize in comparing Christianity with Islam. Because the New Testament says we are to overcome evil with good, while Islam says anyone who resists Islam must be destroyed.

Islam is a church-state, a theocracy, which in all of its manifestations around the world becomes hideously repressive. Show me one country today where Christianity is a theocracy. The answer is: only Tonga, a small island in the Pacific. The fact of the matter is that Christianity in the Reformation brought pluralism to the Western world.

And in America today we have freedom of religion, though a lot of people are trying to chip away at it, unknown before in human history. It is a direct reflection of our belief in the God-given dignity of every human being.

When you compare the histories of Christianity and Islam, even considering the Crusades and the Inquisition, there is no comparison. When you look at the Bible as it is faithfully lived out, there is no comparison. Yes, Christians do bad things just like Muslims do. But there's a fundamental difference. When Christians do them, it's contrary to their belief system. When radical Islamists do them, it is consistent with their belief system.

# A Ticking Time Bomb

Can you believe that the British would allow certain avowed radical Islamists to remain resident in England after the 2005 London Underground bombing?[6] I thought we'd gone soft here, but the British are worse. This was like leaving a ticking time bomb in the middle of a crowded movie theater.

I find that shocking. I find equally shocking an article in the same paper saying, basically, that all Muslims believe in the Koran literally and believe in violence literally, though the Shi'ites have not generally practiced it, nor have the Sunnis. If pressed, they would say that the shedding of blood is necessary for the spread of Islam.

It's interesting that British thinkers, at least, are taking Islam with great seriousness and are looking at it as a clash of civilizations, which most Americans aren't willing to do.

While in Oxford I had a very nice luncheon hosted by David Young, who is president of Oxford Analytica. It is a think tank of sorts, made up of Oxford dons who get together every morning at 8:00 a.m., review the world's events, and put out a newsletter by 11:00 a.m. that goes out all over the world by Internet. It's a fascinating operation.

David had at the lunch the editor of the journal, and both he and another employee of David's, who is a former member of parliament, were asked by those of us sitting around the table at lunch, mostly religious leaders from America but including Alistair McGrath from Oxford, what the major problems were in the world today.

Both men said Islam, that the situation was very grave, and much more serious than people are taking it, that history is repeating itself and we're in for a long, long struggle with militant Islam. These men didn't talk of Islamo-fascism; they talked of militant Islam.

The second thing they said, which was quite interesting, I thought, is that while Western civilization was in decay—that was a given with both of them—the state of the Christian church is very promising. It is growing and having increasing influence all around the world.

The editor of the journal said that he had a specific interest in China because he had lived there a number of years, and that the evidence now is that there are more Chinese Christians than there are Chinese communists. He sees Christianity exploding in China. He supported some of the things that David Aikman has said about the ambitions of the Chinese church.[7] He sees China becoming the other major power in the world, and becoming more Christianized, perhaps, than the West. Wouldn't you like to be alive a couple of generations from now to see how that plays out?

These two men didn't say it, but you could certainly deduce from what they said that they supported what we're doing in Iraq. We didn't have a long enough conversation or I would have asked them that, because how else do you battle Islam than to plant democracies? But something has to happen to wake us up.

If the bombing in London doesn't wake us up enough to throw radical Islamists out of the country, what is going to do it?

# Who's Against Violence?

Pope Benedict says that violence is contrary to reason and religion, and that violence is contrary to the nature of God. All religious leaders—Islamic, Buddhist, Jewish, Christian, Hindu—should affirm that.

The reaction of the Islamic world was to focus on a text from six hundred years ago that was used by the pope to simply explain the context of the historic struggles between Islam and the West. If anyone reads the entire speech by Pope Benedict, he would have to realize that it is an invitation to a sincere effort to bring faiths together, but around certain central truths that all God-loving people should affirm.

The pope has correctly figured out that what is inflaming Islamic sensitivities is the radical secularism of the West. If you read writers like Sayyid Qutb, you realize that what has caused Islamic hatred of us is our decadence. So what the pope is saying is that Christianity has to provide the civilizing, humanizing basis for Europe. If Europe, and eventually America, fall into rampant secularism, this is going to inflame the anger of the Islamic world. Secularism is no match for radical Islam. So the pope is trying to reinvigorate a Christian spirit in Europe and in the West. Peace-loving Muslims should love this.

The problem here is that when the pope condemned violence as contrary to the nature of God, instead of agreeing, the Islamic world responded with violence, thus proving the pope's point. A *Newsweek* article shortly after the pope's speech—an article which wasn't sympathetic with the pope—caught exactly what was going on here. And this is what the Muslim world needs to understand.[8]

When Iran's president, Mahmoud Ahmadinejad, came to America, he was given total freedom of speech and was covered in our press completely. His speech at the United Nations was every bit as provocative against the West as the pope's was, and there wasn't a single demonstration or protest or act of violence in America.

Admadinejad denied the Holocaust, which is a proven historical fact, and spoke about wiping Israel off the map and about America being the great Satan. He also condoned much of the radical violence taking place through terrorist groups. Iran, after all, is funding Hamas and Hezbollah and makes no bones about it.

The contrast of the Western reaction to Ahmadinejad to the Muslim reaction to the pope makes our point. In the West, we listen to Islamic rhetoric and respect the right of Ahmadinejad to say it before the United Nations. We believe in free speech. When Pope Benedict makes statements that are, in my opinion, less inflammatory than Ahmadinejad's, Islam is up in arms.

# The 10 Percent

I am really shaken by what appears to be happening in the Middle East. Islamist parties are winning elections in Egypt and Tunisia, and threaten to win in Libya. So what does this tell us?

Point number one is the West did much to encourage the Arab Spring revolutions in Egypt, Yemen, Tunisia, and Libya. It's understandable why we did. Tyrants were ruling those nations, brutalizing people, and the populace arose in an almost spontaneous revolution. It was widely labeled in the press as a democratic revolution, and everybody hoped that would be the case.

But alas, it's beginning to look like we're exchanging one set of bad guys for another set of bad guys, which raises serious questions about whether Islam is or can be a force for peace in the world.

I have frequently quoted Samuel Huntington in his classic article and book in the 1990s entitled *The Clash of Civilizations*. His premise was that two of the great cultural and religious blocs in the world, the various states of Islam and the various nations of Western civilization, would eventually clash in the twenty-first century. He also predicted that Islam, because it is monolithic and aggressive, would likely win. That part of his prophecy I have consistently rebutted with the assertion that God is sovereign.

After I started talking about this, I got a lot of people very upset. They thought I was casting all of the Muslim world in a negative light. That wasn't true; I've always described it as a "movement of Islamo-fascism" which accounts for about 10 percent of the Muslim population in the world.

The problem is that the 10 percent, the Islamo-fascists, or the radical Islamists, whatever you choose to call them, are the only really organized movement within the Muslim world. So while I am eager to treat Muslims with respect and to welcome efforts at building better relationships with Muslim nations and communities, the only viable organizations within the Muslim world are those like the Muslim Brotherhood, or the Islamo-fascist wing. These are the political activists; these are the people active in the overthrow of governments in Egypt, Libya, and Tunisia. So they inevitably rise to power.

I would love to believe that I'm wrong, and I say this with no disrespect to the vast majority of Muslims who are peace-loving. But so long as radical Islamists can seize political control, there will never be democracy in the Muslim world.

I feel badly for the people in these countries because they really want freedom, but the religious extremists control the levers of power. Eventually tyrants take over, eventually the people rebel, and back come the Islamists.

Now what does this tell us? First, this says to us as Christians that the most important thing we can be doing is evangelizing Muslims. Support missionaries around the world who are doing this. Make every effort to reach out in love to Muslims. We've been doing this in the prisons for twenty years. Okay, we've been doing it with limited success, but it's certainly worth doing.

Second, we as Christians and particularly Americans should do nothing to foster tension between the Muslim world and the liberal democracies of the West. But when it comes to developing policies, it would be the ultimate act of political naïveté to believe that radical Islamists, who believe in theocracy, will ever accept democracy.

Policy-wise, I hope American leaders will begin to look at the Muslim world with a fresh set of realistic lenses. Just overthrowing a dictator like Mubarak, or even a dreadful tyrant like Kaddafi, is not going to solve the problem if we end up with a theocratic Islamist regime in their places. That's known as swapping one tyrant for another.

From a Christian standpoint, we have to see the world realistically. There is a clash of civilizations. That doesn't mean we should be at war with Muslim nations. It means we should be hardheadedly realistic about where we throw our political support.

Worldviews matter. There is an irreconcilable difference between a Christian worldview and the Muslim Brotherhood's worldview. And so long as the Muslim Brotherhood is in the ascendency, we have to be extremely cautious and deliberate about the extent to which we intervene in the affairs of other nations.

Most of the reporters have been talking about the Arab Spring being a great outbreak of the people's desire for freedom. Yes, I think it is that. But I hope it will be another lesson for us, and that is to think twice before we intervene in the affairs of a Muslim uprising.

Idealistically, we would like to think that supporting any revolution that brings about popular rule is going to be a good thing, but then we have to look at Hamas in Palestine, the Muslim Brotherhood in Egypt, and the Ennahda in Tunisia. It's a cautionary but very realistic kind of lesson that we draw from the Arab Spring.

## Loving Our Neighbors

I was not asked to sign the Common Word letter, a Christian-Muslim interfaith initiative, probably because my opposition to signing it was well known by the people organizing the effort.[9] When the invitation was issued by the imams in the first instance, I advised Christians to approach it very warily.

First of all, as evangelicals we have to be a bit humble here. We've only dealt with Islam in the last two hundred years and actually have had little engagement. The Roman Catholic Church, on the other hand, has been engaged in a struggle with Islam since the seventh century and has had a great deal of experience responding to Islamic dialogues. So I told Rick Warren and others to look for the Vatican's reaction before plunging in.

The Vatican remains, to this day, silent about the dialogue, no response to the imams.

The second point that I think is critical is that we should never go into dialogue with anyone when that party is engaged in violence against innocent civilians. If you want to read a really superb paper on this, read Pope Benedict's message at Regensburg.[10] You may remember he was criticized sharply in the press—and there were Islamic protests—because he had talked about Islam's commitment to violence, quoting an earlier church figure.

But the whole point was that violence is contrary to the nature of God, something we can know by evident reason. In other words, Christians and non-Christians alike, including Muslims, should know that violence is an offense to God. So any dialogue, this one or any other, must start with the proposition that both sides renounce violence, repent of violence in the past, and establish that as a fundamental beginning point for any negotiation, or even discussion. I have said this repeatedly to imams I know or have met, and to this day I've never heard moderate Muslims denounce the violence of the terrorists. Maybe they have, but it just hasn't come to my attention. Even this appeal of the imams, responded to by the folks at Yale Divinity School and others, does not make that a precondition, or even mention it.

But even if that precondition had been met, I would not have signed the statement that appeared in a full-page ad in the *New York Times* as the evangelical response.[11] It was fawning, obsequious, and terribly defensive. And why should we be willing to discuss the second great commandment if we're not prepared to discuss the first? Finding common ground on the basis that we ought to love our neighbors is not enough, especially while some Islamists are loving their neighbors so much they're blowing them up.

# 9

## JUDICIAL
## USURPATION

# End Run around Democracy

One of the biggest worries I have at the moment is that the courts are taking over what has historically been the job of the legislature. Why does that matter? It matters greatly because this nation was set up as a self-governing republic; that is, the people agreed to be governed. That's where we get the phrase "the consent of the governed." And ultimately, of course, the sovereignty is with the people. We know of course that it's with God, but from a political structure, it's intended to be vested in the people themselves, which is why, when you go into a courtroom, you hear someone announce, "The people versus so-and-so."

Once judges, who are for the most part unelected, begin to take over the legislative process, they are denying people the right to govern themselves. They're basically taking it away from them. Actually, whether they're elected or not is immaterial. So I have a tendency to be very nervous over the judicial usurpation of legislative power. I think it's always a dangerous trend.

It's been a growing one in America. Liberals figured out forty years ago that if they couldn't get the people to pass the laws the liberals wanted them to pass, they would go to the courts and have them force the legislatures to do it. It was an end run around the legislative process. We saw this with all the lawsuits brought by the legal services corporation and other entities trying to force public policy through the courts.

One of the best examples of that was a statement by Ruth Bader Ginsburg. She was asked about the Equal Rights Amendment, I think when she was speaking at the University of Virginia a few years ago. She said she would still like to have it pass as a symbolic thing for her granddaughter, but it was no longer necessary because the courts had done through various decisions all the things that had originally been in the ERA that was turned down by voters.[1]

There you have it. The voters decided against doing something, but the courts, in effect, did it anyway.

*Roe v. Wade*, of course, falls into this category. The public was debating in every state legislature what policy should be toward the most contentious moral issue of our day. The Supreme Court came along and simply took that away from the people with predictable results. In a self-governing republic, the people don't sit still for this. We still believe that the best form of government is a republic in which the people can pass laws that conform to their own moral traditions. This was Aquinas's view: that the law is nothing but a reflection of the moral consensus. It also was the thing that Calvin argued hard for in the Reformation. I would argue that it has major implications from a biblical perspective.

# A Constitutional Confrontation

I've just read a *New York Times* article titled "A Turf Battle's Unlikely Victim."[2] It was an in-depth piece on the aftermath of the Miranda case.

I personally think that the court came to the right conclusion in *Miranda*, largely on the basis that judicial practice had established this for so long that it would be disruptive to change it.

The bombshell part of the decision was not that they upheld *Miranda*, which I expected them to do, but rather, that they used the decision to further advance their argument that *only* the Supreme Court has the right to say what is constitutional. This is the very argument that many of us tackled in the "End of Democracy?" symposium in *First Things* in 1997. We argued that if the court believed this, the court was wrong constitutionally. That Congress was having its powers usurped and that we were in a great constitutional crisis.

I talked with the late Henry Hyde about this in the 1990s in connection with the Religious Liberties Protection Act.[3] Hyde agreed and Canady agreed—but beyond these two men we could find very few people on Capitol Hill who even realized, let alone cared, that the Supreme Court was digging Congress's foundations out one by one, a shovel full at a time.[4]

Up until now, it has been a matter of our interpreting this as the court's strategy. The court hasn't really come out and said so, but in Rehnquist's opinion they are explicit. They went right back and traced it to the first decision, *Marbury v. Madison*, from which the right of judicial review was deduced as the result of a court precedent, not of anything explicit in the Constitution. And Rehnquist went on to use the dispute over religious liberty as his case study in point. *This is frightening.*

I think we once again have to sound the alarm. Maybe nobody will listen; maybe the Congress is willing to throw in the towel and surrender their authority; maybe we're witnessing the end of self-government as we know it, but I can't be quiet.

I'd like to freshen up my old *End of Democracy* arguments — which I made at great length, and which we also turned into a document called "We Hold These Truths" — and apply them to what is now the court's explicit declaration that it has taken over this power and that Congress has no right to interfere.

In another time in American history, this would have created a huge constitutional crisis. But this Congress, I'm sorry to say, is dead asleep. They don't care. They're raising money, feathering their nests, protecting their position, and they couldn't care less about great constitutional questions.

Why this became so important to Christians is that we have always viewed the law as a reflection of the moral consensus of the people. This point was made by Augustine and Aquinas. It is central to Blackstone's arguments about the law. The law merely reflects the moral traditions of the people, but the essence of self-government is for people to be able to express these moral traditions in the law. If they do so, they pass something like the Religious Freedom Restoration Act or Proposition Two in Colorado a few years ago, and then the court comes along and says you have no right to pass that. You have no right to enact your moral traditions in the law. In fact, in the *Romer v. Evans* case, which struck down Proposition Two, the court went so far as to tell the voters of Colorado that in passing the proposition they were reflecting animus toward homosexuals. Utterly preposterous!

# The Rule of Law—or of Lawyers?

The rule of law is a fundamentally Christian proposition. It really broke through in the West because of Samuel Rutherford's *Lex Rex*. That was the first idea we had that said the king wasn't the supreme authority, the law was.

Now having said that, it's only fair to point out that in the Hebrew and Christian cultures, there is an understanding about the supremacy of the law. The problem was that it was mediated by the king, or in the case of the Catholic Church, by the pope. Law was always considered a transcendent authority and there was always a history and tradition of natural law, so we have to be careful we don't put all the emphasis on Rutherford. That was a breakthrough in the Reformation. But I've given any number of talks and written articles on this subject. The rule of law goes back and has roots in the Jews. Michael Novak has argued that; so has Paul Johnson. So the Christian understanding is that the law is an absolute. It's law because it's law, not because we say it is.

Lawyers are now taking a very different point of view. They're accomplishing through litigation what can't be done legislatively. Now if people expressly accept laws being imposed by courts, this is because of the aggressiveness of lawyers and the loss of the understanding of the rule of law. But what this is going to cost us is democracy; judicial usurpation as a result of lawyers' agitation results in the loss of self-government.

I've written about this repeatedly and we've got to keep writing about it, talking about it.

# A Puff of Smoke

It is specious of our opponents to argue that if the states outlaw gay "marriage" then we don't need a Federal Marriage Amendment. That's what even some supporters are saying.

We forget the Defense of Marriage Act and all the state constitutions and all of the state referenda would go up in a puff of smoke with one court decision, a Supreme Court decision that said under the Fourteenth Amendment that the rights of gays to "marry" is constitutionally protected—equal treatment under the law.

The court would hold that tomorrow if the issue were before them. I say it because they did this with *Roe v. Wade.* I say it because they've gone farther into judicial activism even since *Roe v. Wade*, particularly the *Lawrence* case in 2003, and later with the 2005 case that ruled it is cruel and unusual punishment to execute a teenager.

Notice that the court relied on European precedents in the 2005 case as they did in the *Lawrence* case. So the court would feel free to look at the fact that European nations are allowing gay "marriage" with no ill effects. That's what they would say. Of course, the ill effects are grievous and demonstrable. But just imagine trying to argue that in the Supreme Court. The court, as it is presently constituted, would find gay "marriage" constitutionally protected.

Then the job of getting a defense of marriage amendment passed would be virtually impossible, because you would be taking away a right, which the court is always reluctant to do. You would be, by constitutional amendment, reversing the court, which to my knowledge, off the top of my head, has only happened in the case of slavery.

In other words, the whole opposition to the Federal Marriage Amendment is based on a premise that gay "marriage" can be stopped other ways. It can't be. Gay "marriage" is with us unless we've got the guts to pass this amendment and pass it quickly, which by the way, two-thirds of the American people want. I don't understand why politicians are timid. I think it's that they really want to have things both ways. They want to be in favor of heterosexual marriage, but they don't want to offend gays. On this case, they've got to choose, and we've got to force them to choose, and sooner rather than later. If we wait until the court acts, we're finished.

# "In Your Face" with the Courts

I talked at great length with Congressman Charles Canady a couple of months after the Supreme Court overturned the Religious Freedom Restoration Act (RFRA) in 1997. The House had just adjourned and he had plenty of time on his hands, and we spent about forty-five minutes on the phone.

This guy is simply terrific. He understands the issues. He is smart, judicious, and determined to win. His strategy is to hold hearings during which he brings in experts on a variety of subjects so that he can begin to build momentum. His preference is then to come out with a bill that draws on the federal funding power and the commerce clause to simply rewrite RFRA, basing it on that authority. He thinks he could get that through both the House and the Senate early next year. [Actually, it would take until 2000 for the Religious Land Use and Institutionalized Persons Act to be passed unanimously in Congress.]

But it all depends on grassroots support. The Congress is lethargic. They are not going to get involved in the issue even though there's a question of their institutional authority at stake. Canady did say that all the faith communities have responded and are strong on this. But like everything else in today's environment, it could become a big, hot issue one day and disappear the next.

We also know that the media is giving us no help, so this is one of those campaigns that is going to require massive grassroots, Christian organization from every resource we have.

Canady also told me that another congressman has a resolution to propose that would put the Congress on record as refusing to recognize RFRA.[5] Canady is uncertain about that. He is very much afraid of it being "in your face" with the court. He thinks that will only harden them, cause them to reverse the next statute, and keep the issue in flux for years to come.

I emphasized with him how important it was to preserve the three coordinate, coequal branches of government, and that Congress has as much to say about constitutional interpretation as the court. I argued that the institutional principle was at stake and that the whole future of self-government depended on how it was resolved.

He understands this. He also understands that a constitutional amendment would be a catastrophe. The only exception to that, he said, is if he could get a constitutional amendment passed that would teach the court that they couldn't mess with the Congress, and that if they did, the people would respond, rise up, and amend the Constitution. He thought that would put them in their place for generations. I disagreed and told him so. He recognizes, however, that you would never get this particular amendment through the state legislatures. The states would not want to be bound by federal standards. So he understands that the legislative route is the only one.

I was impressed that Canady is very cautious, careful, deliberate, and he thinks these issues through. I'm much more impulsive and rash than he is. But we're on exactly the same wavelength.

There's an interesting observation here on the sovereignty of God. For many years, when people asked Canady why he was in politics, he would say, "I feel called as a Christian to be in politics and defend religious liberty." He said he was never quite sure why he said that because there weren't many religious liberty issues that were that major that he was involved in, but he kept feeling that that was why God wanted him in politics.

He said when he got the chairmanship of the House Subcommittee on the Constitution, he realized he would be dealing with religious liberty questions but never imagined it would be something like RFRA, the biggest religious liberty issue of the past century. But it's obvious God had a pattern for his life, prepared him, gave him a concern for religious liberty, made him a skilled lawyer and state legislator, and now has put him in a position where a great religious liberty issue will come before his committee. Extraordinary.

# 10

## BLESSED ARE
## the POOR

## Smashing Idols

One of the great distinctives about the ministry of Prison Fellowship is that we are targeted toward not only the poor, who obviously have a special place in God's heart, but the poorest of the poor: the prisoner. He's helpless, powerless, has no resources, no freedom. He has been stripped of everything, which, when you come right down to it, is the best definition of *poor*. It's true that Prison Fellowship's witness goes way beyond that, and that we speak on worldview issues and all the rest of it, but the heart of this ministry is to reach the poorest of the poor.

I've been reflecting a lot lately and have come to realize that this gets us very close to God, and He seems to favor us. I'm dictating these words on the thirtieth anniversary of my own conversion, and this is one of the thoughts that have been rolling through my mind now for weeks. These thoughts were given some impetus by a marvelous message I heard on ministering to the poor by Tim Keller at Redeemer Presbyterian Church in New York City.

Why is there such an emphasis on the poor all through Scripture? Is it because Jesus is sorry for the poor? Yes, maybe in one sense there's a special concern for the poor because they have been left out. But I think it goes to something much more central to the Christian faith than that.

You have to really understand what being poor is. It doesn't just mean you're living below the poverty level or that you are hungry for your next meal. It means that you are absolutely powerless. You have no human resources. You've just been released from prison. You have twenty-five or a hundred dollars, a bus ticket home, an old suit of clothes, and there you are, no friends, no place you can go. Nobody will take you in; nobody wants you. Where do you turn?

I think about older prisoners who are totally forgotten. They're in prison for life, and when they die, nobody claims their body. At the Louisiana State Penitentiary at Angola, the Christian warden, Burl Cain, has built a cemetery. Prisoners who die are given a horse-drawn funeral procession. He's gone to great lengths to give some dignity to the burial.

Prisoners may get food and have a place to sleep, but they are totally vulnerable. Anybody can do anything they want to them, and they can't defend themselves.

So why would Jesus say that the kingdom of heaven belongs to the poor? Is it because they've been so badly treated during this life? No. I think it is because the really poor have no human means to sustain themselves and are therefore without any idols. Nothing interferes with their total devotion to God and their trust in him.

What happens to the rest of us? We have, as Keller puts it, a middle-class spirit. Yes, we want Jesus to redeem us from our sins and give us eternal bliss in his company. But we're not totally dependent on Christ right now, not by a long shot. We've got our 401ks and retirement funds, and when the car develops an oil leak, we trade it in. Another month, we take some money to buy more furniture, put up new draperies. I for one have a hundred distractions every day that take my mind away from total trust in God. As hard as I try not to, I have many, many idols.

Luke talks about being poor. I think he defines poverty as having nothing. The translation in Matthew from the Beatitudes, however, is "poor in spirit." Could it be that Jesus is telling us to emulate the poor—that is, we should seek to be like them? As Keller says, we should get rid of our middle-class spirit and adopt the spirit of the poor. We should find that purity of love and relationship with Jesus. The poor have no choice. We do have a choice, but by choice we should embrace the spirit of the poor. We should become poor in spirit.

I'm grateful to the Lord, particularly as I reflect on these thirty years, that He's given me such extraordinary opportunities to witness to the powerful and the powerless alike, to engage the church in the great cultural struggles of our day and to promote a biblical worldview. But I'm especially thankful that he has brought me a ministry to the poor, and I, like every pilgrim, am struggling to be truly poor in spirit. I'm thankful for the examples I see of this all around me when I visit prisons.

Norman Podhoretz, in his book *The Prophets: Who They Were, What They Are,* argues that the prophets believed idolatry was a form of self-deification. That's exactly what idolatry is: it's the idea that we're God ourselves, and we make ourselves idols. And it's as Podhoretz put it: a delusion that humans could become as gods and make the world in our own image, which, of course, as he sees it, is the same phenomena that has taken place in modern American life. Liberalism believes that people can, on their own, arrive at utopian conclusions and judgments. This is the ultimate idolatry. So modern liberalism, which wants the government to not impose any moral code on us whatsoever because we can create our own, is just a matter of idolatry. It's the same kind of idolatry that the prophets railed against, and it's the same kind of idolatry that takes us away from God and contrasts us with the poor, who have all of these pretensions of power and influence stripped away and, therefore, are just hungry to know God.

In his monumental work on Genesis, Leon Kass sees the same thing. He talks about the unbounded ambitions of modern "democratic man." One consequence of these ambitions is he says that "the project of Babel has been making a comeback," as science and technology threaten a "human imperium over nature."[1]

I've never thought in these terms before, but this is what the Bible warns against. This is what modern culture is doing and the Bible offers us a model: Be poor in spirit. We become poor in spirit when we embrace the attitude of the poor, which is to rely on nothing and to trust totally in God—to smash idols.

# God's Upside-down Kingdom

As a believer, one is drawn to the Beatitudes as a formula for the good, fulfilling life. After all, they are Jesus' central message about the kingdom of God. Isn't this the sort of thing that tells us how we should be living our lives? And of course, Christians read the two accounts—one in Matthew and one in Luke—and go away shaking their heads or feeling frustrated, realizing they could never live that way.

I hear more rationalizations of the Beatitudes than of any other parts of Scripture, and I myself wrestled with this in *God and Government*. I dealt with it in the book, I believe, in the only reasonable way you can; that is, by saying that the Beatitudes are values by which people will live in the coming kingdom. We should be aspiring to them now, in our personal lives, but they aren't the values that govern day-to-day conduct in a fallen world. Jesus is giving us a preview, if you will, of what it looks like in the kingdom.

But I am increasingly of the mind that Jesus really does mean to give us certain personal characteristics that we should be striving for in this life. He's giving us some of the secrets to the good life. If you mourn, you are going to be comforted. If you are meek, you will inherit the earth (the great paradox again: the weak and humble rise to the top in God's upside-down kingdom). You should hunger and thirst after righteousness; you'll find it. You should be merciful, and you'll be shown mercy. You should be pure in heart. You should be peacemakers. You should be willing to be persecuted for righteousness. These are all good qualities to strive for as we live our lives.

The hang-up comes, of course, on the very first one: "Blessed are the poor in spirit," Jesus says in Matthew 5:3. Then, in Luke 6:20, he says, "Blessed are you who are poor, for yours is the kingdom of God." Everybody I've ever heard speak on this subject gravitates toward the Matthew translation because you can talk about being poor in spirit as being humble. And all of us should be humble and meek and not be taken over by pride. I've never heard anybody talk about being *poor*. I've never heard anybody talk about *poor* meaning poverty until I heard a sermon by Tim Keller. I won't try to develop his whole argument, but his conclusion is that the poor must be our primary concern, that God really does have a preference for the poor.

Tim describes poverty as being helpless, defenseless, having no friends, and being totally without power. You're a single mom, you're trying to raise three kids, you're in a ghetto, you're paying rent to somebody who could throw you out tomorrow, and no one would care if they did. He defines it, in other words, as something more than just lack of money: it's a lack of ability to do anything to improve your life; it is utter, abject rejection. It is for those people that God calls us to show a special concern.

But why would God single out the poor? What makes poverty a virtuous quality? Why would the poor inherit the kingdom of heaven?

Tim doesn't get to the same point I want to make here, but he develops the argument nicely that there is something to being poor. All Christians try to be in the world but not of it—to acquire possessions to live a better life, to see their kids get better educated than they were, and hopefully make more money and live more comfortably. This is the great American dream.

The problem is that for all of us these things become idols. And the one thing the poor have going for them is that every idol has been stripped away. They have nothing they can rely on. They have been stripped naked of all the things that the world holds to be of value, so that they are free to worship Christ with no distractions. They are free to focus on what really matters in life. They are free to find a wonderful, joy-filled experience with God.

I'm not advocating that people get rid of all their possessions and give their house away and go live in the streets and sever all relationships so they haven't got any friends who could help them or feed them. That, of course, would be preposterous. And if every Christian did this, the world would collapse and the gospel wouldn't get spread, so it simply doesn't work.

The point is, however, we have to be prepared to think that way, and I think that is what Jesus is teaching. We have to seek total freedom from idolatry around us. The poor have it because it is forced on them. It's not a good thing; it's not something I'd want to go out and advocate. But they, in one sense, can be closer to God.

Could this be what Mother Teresa had in mind when she said,

"We'll never know how much we owe the poor until we get to heaven"? If this analysis is correct, the poor can bless us, and we ourselves can be blessed in a way that is so countercultural that it defies understanding.

I've had glimpses of this blessing from time to time. Because I didn't want my kids to have a distorted view of life by taking them to all the nice places in the world for vacations and giving them a trip to Europe for their graduation present, that kind of thing, I took my three kids to Lima, Peru, to visit all of Mike Timmis's projects. It's really quite amazing, in the midst of incredible squalor, to see how people can rise above it and live good lives. We met dozens of people that weekend who, in your heart of hearts, you might actually envy because they have a dignity about them and a faith that's deeper than I ever experienced on Sunday mornings in church.

I remember one particular family that drives this point home. Mike Timmis, former chairman of the board of Prison Fellowship, ran mini-enterprise funds in Peru. Somebody could be sold a bicycle worth $100 and start making deliveries and pay back the $100. He took us to visit one of those people who had started a little business at his home. The circumstances are such that it becomes a very vivid, telling metaphor. These were uneducated people who had come in from the bush to live in the city. Peru has tens of thousands of homemade shacks that are built anywhere squatters can put them, and they line the hillsides all around the cities of Peru. They're sometimes called *barrios*, but basically they are homes people built for themselves. They get scrap materials, find bricks and stones. They build a wall and eventually have a thatched roof. Some go two stories. Some are quite good. It's an extraordinary testimony to human resourcefulness and the need of human beings to shelter their families and protect one another. They've built enormous communities—dirt roads, no running water. But the homes are surprisingly good. It may take them years to get it built. They get menial jobs, pick up money wherever they can, scavenge around, and build these houses.

The big problem, of course, is getting land to do this on. They'll start building on a hillside and the owner will come and drive them off. One of the places they've been able to settle a little mini city is on top of what was once the garbage dump of all of Lima. This community is built right on top of the garbage dump. We went to a medical clinic set up by Mike that was giving people shots and treatments and medicines, a marvelous thing right on top of this garbage dump. Then Mike took us to this man who had gotten a $100 loan to start a waste management business. What he does is go around the ghettos collecting stray bottles and pieces of paper and then brings them back to his house. In the yard he separates all of the trash he collects. He bundles it, and he sells it to truckers who pick it up. He makes what is for that area a decent living so that he's able to feed and clothe his family and keep his kids in school.

To an outsider, it's unbelievable squalor. His home has a dirt floor, no running water, a hole in the ground for toilets. The water comes from a cistern outside; they have to buy it and bring it into the house in buckets.

The husband is a hard-working Peruvian of Indian ancestry. He met us at the front door, actually in his courtyard. I stuck out my hand to shake his, and he held out his elbow instead. His hands were dirty, and this was his way of presenting himself in a more desirable way. I was struck by how sensitive he was about this.

I was also struck by how much dignity this family maintained living in a hut on top of a garbage dump. When my daughter Emily started to take a picture of a couple of the kids because they were so cute, the mother, that is, the man's daughter, came out, grabbed a ladle with some of the precious water, and washed her kids' faces before Emily took the picture.

I'm convinced human dignity is not related to our economic circumstances. These people had a desire to look well, to present themselves well. They had self-respect even though they lived in circumstances most of us couldn't imagine. Here they were huddled together in this house and yet smiling and vibrant, excited to see us. We had a prayer with them. They were filled with joy, absolutely amazed, so proud of their home and so proud of their job, and so proud of the fact that they were self-sufficient. They were able to run this business and keep their family together. There must have been fifteen of them, the husband and wife, their children and grandchildren, all living in this one place with virtually no amenities, but they had dignity.

"Blessed are the poor, for theirs is the kingdom of heaven." These people understood something, frankly, that a lot of people in the world don't today. They were grateful to be alive, grateful they could have their dignity, grateful they could know their God and worship Him, and were unencumbered by all the junk and heavy baggage that so burdens many people in the world today.

We should be making every effort humanly possible to end poverty. We should be looking for every way we possibly can to improve the lives of people who live in poverty. But at the same time, we ought to recognize that those who do live in poverty often present a lesson for us because they have found the most fundamental good things in life: dignity, self-respect, love of God.

I saw this exact same phenomenon in the Philippines when I visited a pedi-cab project. It's a story I've told many times, of meeting with ex-offenders who came out of the Manalupa prison. Each one had a pedi-cab and started a mini enterprise. This was in a slum far worse than what I saw in Peru, but a beautiful moment came when I was sitting there and saw this little girl jump up on the stage. The ex-offenders were singing to us, a group of visitors from the West. Their families were all down front, and it was a makeshift platform in a little open area where the pedi-cabs gathered. This little girl jumped up on the platform, went over to her father, and hugged him around the legs and looked up in his eyes so adoringly as he caressed her hair. I'll never forget the scene because I thought to myself that it's worth everything I do in this ministry just to see that person finding that joy.

So, I think I understand what Tim Keller is talking about. I think I understand what Jesus was talking about. "Blessed are the poor, for theirs is the kingdom of heaven," and they have found something in all of their difficulties that's hard for us to see. You can see why it's harder for a rich man to enter the kingdom of heaven than the poor. You can see why the rich young ruler walked away; he couldn't give up all these things that are idolatrous.

Again, this is the paradox: lose your life for Christ's sake to find it, don't be distracted by the things of this world. You have to get rid of false idols.

We must try to lead people to understand the truth of the moral order, to understand the paradox of life, to understand where true meaning comes from, to understand how gratitude motivates us to do things, to understand what fulfills us. And one of the things we have to deal with is false idols. Everybody has them, and the uncanny part of Jesus' teaching is that He is really telling us to strip all of these away and to think a whole new way about reality. It is counterintuitive, countercultural, but it is true.

This really, as you think about it, is the ultimate paradox: What you think you want most is what, in fact, you want least. This is why John Wesley used to give away everything he had at the end of every year and start fresh in the new year so that he was totally dependent upon God.

## Civic Responsibility—For All

I met with a prominent businessman in New York last weekend, and we talked about the economic situation. It was interesting how close my assessment was to his. He's in the business world and should know what's going on if anybody really does.

One of the things he told me that I thought was fascinating was that we have a totally dysfunctional tax system because half the population is not paying any federal income tax. Of course, when that happens you can never cut the budget. And that really is the source of the problem.

His argument, which was new to me, is that the way we're behaving is very demeaning to the poor. We're saying to them, "you're poor; you can't carry your own weight as a citizen, so we'll subsidize you." Not only does that feed the entitlement mentality, which we got into a great discussion about, but it makes poor people feel as though they're servants of the state. It's demeaning.

I'm talking about spreading the responsibility of paying for government, certainly with a progressive tax system, but with no one excluded. And even if someone only paid $50 or $25 a year, at least they would be making some investment in the government. They would have some interest in how the government performs. They would have a little more concern for the responsibility of our expenditures. It would cultivate what was once the cardinal civic virtue—that is, civic duty and individual responsibility.

I also wonder, if justice is the goal of government, whether it is just to exempt half the people from paying taxes. Justice is about everyone getting their due. It means that everybody pays their fair share; it means that everybody is subject to punishment if they violate the law. To segregate half the people out and say that they're not part of the tax base, it seems to me, is not just. It's not just to those who do pay taxes; it's not just to the overall goals of the system. And it is downright patronizing. I was very impressed with the arguments of the businessman I met.

We know for sure that we're very close to the tipping point. And when you go over it, you cannot pass laws cutting expenditures; it's impossible, because half the people are just recipients. The other half who are the givers pay the bills. It's really giving the benefits of citizenship without any responsibilities, which is wrong.

# Poppies and the Poor

I've just read a Ross Douthat column in the *New York Times*. It's one of the best I've read in a while. He absolutely nails it. What he's basically saying is that we can tax people more and that may reduce their income. In that sense it levels them down; he describes it as cutting off the tallest poppies in the field. But it can't fix a broken government.

The government is broken, and we have what he calls a new "Eden" class, which is the public sector employees who are living off the fat of the land and doing a miserable job of taking care of the poor. He doesn't say this, but that's precisely what happened in the Communist revolution. It was class warfare. The Russian royals and the wealthy classes had been soaking the poor, so it was off with their heads. And in came the new guys, the reformers, who very shortly became powerful, entrenched, and wealthy. So it went from a monarchy to a tyranny, with the people at the top still feeding off the backs of the poor. Only someone who believes in original sin and the fall can fully understand this.

Douthat is raising the most potent question that needs to be addressed. The system we are living with and working with, the relationship between the private and public sector, the whole question of the purpose of government—these are the issues that have to be addressed before you can decide who taxes who for what. It's not a revenue problem; it is a disastrous misallocation of our resources that is transferring so-called wealth generation from the private to the public sector, where none will be generated. It's going against at least a thousand years of human experience.

Douthat's column makes one very powerful point. But we need to make another. How do Christians really look at this? First of all, we know of government and taxes what Jesus told us: to render to Caesar what is Caesar's and to God what is God's. There was a tax system at the time of the New Testament. It was all corrupt; the most corrupt people were the tax collectors; they just took it for themselves. So government has not changed that much in two thousand years.

The second point is that government's job remains to preserve order, do justice, and restrain evil. We're to collect funds for the common defense, common needs, general public health and welfare. But there's a long Christian tradition here of subsidiarity and sphere sovereignty that limits government. During the Reformation it was a republic that was considered the ideal form of government. Never was it thought that government would take care of all the people all of the time and meet all their needs or that we would have anything like a socialist state. The Bible is very clear, and Christian tradition is even clearer, in the respect for private property.

Three, the Bible has many injunctions for helping the poor. When the Catholic Church has a preferential option for the poor, I understand it. I understand it because the weak and the marginalized in our society are especially close to God's heart. We know that; it's all through the Scripture and particularly in the Old Testament. In the New Testament we see frequent references to helping people in need—widows and orphans. But nowhere—and here's the important point—does it say the government is supposed to do this. These are all instructions for Christians in terms of their individual behavior. Sphere sovereignty and subsidiarity were presented as limitations on the state so that the state wouldn't take over the individual function, because if it does, you stifle people and prevent acts of virtue.

Four, nowhere in the Bible—nor in Christian tradition (other than liberation theology)—is there the idea of redistribution of wealth. In my opinion, quite to the contrary. I will confess to not having a really firm grip on how traditions have dealt with this over the years. So we may find there are some Christian schools of thought that have made such arguments. But certainly that wouldn't be doctrine in any one of our churches today. Income redistribution is, as Douthat points out, leveling society down; that is, penalizing certain people and taking money that has been justly earned by one person and giving it to somebody else. Remember, too, the apostle Paul's teaching that if a man doesn't work, don't let him eat. There's a strong work component to the Bible, which would be undermined by any attempt to take money from the rich and give it to the poor. That's Robin Hood; that's not the Bible.

Five, envy is a sin, whereas helping your neighbor is a virtue, and loving your neighbor is demanded by Christianity. This whole movement of redistribution of wealth is promoted by a vice.

Six, any tax system has to be fair. The progressive income tax is a very new phenomenon. It's understandable; it has evolved for good, prudential reasons in prosperous industrial nations. And all of us can understand why that is so, because if you have great wealth, you should be paying more in taxes. But we're over the edge today. We've got half the people paying no taxes, so they feel no sense of ownership or burden or responsibility for the state. That is very unhealthy.

Equally unhealthy is to treat taxes as a punitive measure, where we're going to punish certain people because they've made and accumulated all this money. That runs through the rhetoric of the "Occupy Wall Street" movement so strongly that I think we need to deal with it. It is really envy running wild and using the power of the state to punish some for having been too successful. The death tax really does that, as well, which is why so many of us oppose it, even though I can see arguments for it. It's just wrong on principle.

No society can keep its culture intact when the natural vice of envy, which all of us have experienced, gets out of control and gets enforced by law so that the poor can punish the rich.

A tax plan has to be fair: The rich should pay more as a percentage, but the poor should also pay something. Otherwise they feel no sense of responsibility.

I'm not opposed to raising taxes; I think they're going to have to be raised. I think we're going to have to get rid of all corporate welfare, one hundred percent of it. And if more has to be paid by the wealthy to get us out of debt, we'll pay it, but not if it's going to line the pockets of the bureaucratic elite who are governing us today. That's not right.

# Social Justice or ...?

I have been reading about the Occupy Wall Street movement and found the discussion between the Centurions, members of Prison Fellowship's intensive, yearlong Christian worldview course (now called Colson Fellows) interesting and provocative. My view of the Occupy movement is that it was a disparate group of grievance-laden protestors—people who felt they were victims of society in one form or another—and they looked for chances to attack the "system." Some anarchists were mixed in with this; clearly there were communists and socialists involved—you could see it in their posters. It was an odd assortment of malcontents with no real thrust, unless perhaps you could boil it down to what the term *social justice* is commonly understood to mean. That is, redistribution of wealth.

There is a very powerful force in American life today among leftist intellectuals. They aren't pushing for higher taxes for the purpose of raising revenue; they are pushing for higher taxes in order to get income equality enshrined in the law. I'll make a prediction: I bet I'll live long enough to see it come true, although it will make me sad. The next big "rights" campaign will be the right to a "fair share" of national wealth. It will no longer be about just being even-handed with all ethnic groups or not discriminating against certain kinds of behavior or people. It is now an affirmative goal that people will all share abundantly in a nation's wealth. To achieve that, positive steps have to be taken to redistribute. Obama has said this in so many words; so have many of his supporters. And we're hearing it increasingly from the left, and this was the bottom line with the Occupy movement, if there really is a bottom line.

The term *social justice* is really misunderstood. I recommend an article by Michael Novak, "Defining Social Justice," that I found on the *First Things* website. I also strongly recommend the piece Marvin Olasky wrote for the Colson Center "Social Justice vs. Righteous Justice." It's a brilliant exposition of the social justice question.

Let me put it in the simplest terms. The purpose of the Christian is to fulfill the Great Commission and the cultural commission. We are working to the end that people might be saved spiritually and that they might become part of a new community of life in which there is human flourishing, justice, and righteousness. That's our goal. That's what we believe here at the Colson Center. That's what every Christian, I think, should be aiming at.

A consequence of doing this will be social justice. Social justice is a great term. We want social justice. But we don't want what has become a code word for *redistribution*. We want social justice, but not the social justice that has characterized a modern movement about redistribution of wealth.

We're at a really treacherous point in American life today. If the economy turns around, if these signs we're getting in recent days hold forth, we may dodge the bullet. If there's another collapse in the economy, or if left-leaning politicians continue to spend us into bankruptcy, then there will be a crisis, and the only way out of that crisis will be to impose some system of distribution of wealth so that people can survive the crisis. Don't think this isn't already in the minds of a number of our politicians.

So from my perspective, the tragedy that I want to see us avert is all of us sitting around calmly, blissfully expecting things to get better while they're actually getting worse, and suddenly there's a crisis and we've already been mentally conditioned for the idea that out of that crisis has to come a distribution system that is fair to all and takes care of all. That's how the richest, most prosperous nation in human history could back into a form of socialism or worse.

I think it's also important to understand that there's nothing wrong with government raising money for purposes like building roads or libraries or schools. You're quite right, these aren't Marxian evils; these are things that serve the common good, and therefore we should be imposing a fair system of taxation so that all people pay a reasonable share of the burden to achieve them. That is entirely different from legislation that is aimed at "curing" the inequality in income and wealth. It is a very, very hot issue today, just below the surface, however.

The Bible is clear about what the role of government is. It's also clear that government is limited and under the law. Christian tradition is strong on this, particularly in the Reformation. Calvin's argument for a republic is that it would preserve the rule of law but avoid the ultimate evils of the tyranny of a majority.

Both evangelicals, with sphere sovereignty, and Catholics, with subsidiarity, have believed in a limited role for government. It is not to have an all-encompassing role in society, nor is it the ultimate arbiter. It is the judge that keeps things moving in all the other appropriate spheres of human activity.

For local governments to take on building libraries is a totally appropriate thing. It is serving the community needs. It could be done by schools and often is. It could be done by private individuals. But it's never something that is imposed on people. It is either supported through community efforts, voluntary contributions, or by taxation, if the local jurisdiction votes people into office who want to have a public library. I don't see any problem with that. The problem comes when we think that everything has to be justified in Scripture. That gets us into further trouble, because in the Old Testament many of the things that the Jews were commanded to do was part of their covenant with God as the people of God; it wasn't assigned to the government to do. Leaving gleanings on the sides of the fields, for example, was a way in which individuals could behave responsibly and care for the poor. People like Jim Wallis and others frequently cite those passages as justification for the government to care for the poor. Remember that Israel was a theocracy. It was basically the church acting in the place of the state. Those provisions are not necessarily transferable to New Testament times or the modern world.

Of course, government can take many forms. Those living during the Enlightenment believed that the free democratic model was the best kind. I don't think anybody could read the Bible in its entirety and recommend any kind of tyranny or even a severe authoritarian rule.

We have a priority, as Christians, to care for the poor. But I don't think that means we can impose our views on society and force society to do what Scripture clearly teaches is the challenge for the church. At the same time, that doesn't mean that we can't legislate responsibly in the common good to try to be sure that benefits are spread as widely as possible to all citizens and that our common needs are met.

Ken Myers has an interesting interview on his latest Mars Hill tapes on the subject of the close relationship between religion and politics. Religion, coming from the Latin *religare*, means to bind together in pursuit of a common belief. That's how we organize ourselves in society, in pursuit of that belief and in fulfilling that belief system. But politics is how we organize our common lives in the community together, the *polis*. So there's a tremendous overlap, and we need to be sensitive to that. And we need to be sure that government is respecting the right of the free community to do what it has to do, and the free community is supporting the government in doing what it has to do. I think if you keep that perspective in mind you'll come to just conclusions, even if they don't satisfy everyone.

# The One Percent

Everyone is bent out of shape that one percent of the people are making 17 percent of the national income and as much as the entire bottom 50 percent of the population is making. Liberals are loving this because it's making the case for income redistribution. And they are playing class warfare. It's plain and simple.

What is the problem with class warfare? It arises from a violation of the tenth commandment: Thou shalt not covet. It feeds on one of the most vicious public sins—the sin of envy. So politicians today are playing, not to a virtue in life and not promoting a virtue, but promoting a vice. This would be like a political party coming out saying everybody should start drinking to excess or using marijuana or other drugs.

We live in a society which has lost its sense of virtue, which I've been talking about for a long time. One of the signs of that is when we start making an appeal for a vice. It wouldn't solve the problem of poverty if we did have income redistribution, because it would go from the top one percent, not to the people who need it most, but to the governing class who are already a new elite in American life.

In his book, *The Seven Deadly Sins Today*, social critic Henry Fairlie wrote:

> It has been said that envy is the one deadly sin to which no one readily confesses. It seems to be the nastiest, the most grim, the meanest. Sneering, sly, vicious. The face of envy is never lovely. It is never even faintly pleasant. Its expression crosses our faces in a split second. 'Few are able to suppress in themselves the secret satisfaction at the misfortune of their friends,' said La Rochefoucauld, 'and few of us are able to suppress a secret envy at someone else's good fortune, or even at someone else's good joke.' If we confessed each day how often we had been envious during it, we would be on our knees longer than for any of all the other sins.[2]

None of the seven deadly sins are particularly attractive, although a few look attractive when you first start into the practice. Is there anyone who is not envious? Even the super-rich become envious of one another. That's the reason very wealthy people go bankrupt trying to keep up with the rest of the super-elite wealthy class—because they envy them. Somebody else has something they don't have.

I will confess that for a long time I would hear something harmful that had been done to a competitor or some misfortune that someone had, and I'd think *I'm glad that wasn't me* or *Maybe it will take that person out of the way*. If anybody says they haven't envied, they are going to lie about other things as well.

I think focusing on the Tenth Commandment makes this whole question of income redistribution a clear case of Christian interest.

# 11

# PERSECUTION

# Doing Business with the Devil

*Chuck highly valued Roberto Rivera, a* BreakPoint
*writer and thinker extraordinaire who worked with Chuck in various
capacities for some twenty years. At the time this memo was dictated,
Roberto regularly wrote a colorful news summary containing insights
nobody else would have come up with. These entertaining summaries
gave Chuck many an idea for a* BreakPoint *commentary.*

As so often happens, Roberto Rivera has come up with a classic
insight, one you wouldn't find in the *Wall Street Journal* or *Forbes*
magazine or any mainstream press. The reason you wouldn't
find it there is that the mainstream press doesn't want anybody
to know about this. They don't want us to know because it would
cause us to stop trading with certain tyrannical regimes.

The mainstream press with all of their big money advertisers
and their pro-business bias — most of them, at least — don't want
to do anything that closes any market for us. Even when those
markets are tyrannies, even when they're taking prisoners and
shooting them in the back of the head and then harvesting their
organs, as an NBC special revealed that the Chinese are doing.

The timing for Roberto's insight could not be more propitious.
The president of China will be arriving the end of next week in
Washington.[1] President Bill Clinton is anxious to give him a good
reception notwithstanding the fact that the Chinese are chewing up
pastors and burning churches. All of us in the religious community
will be pleading with the president to use this occasion to pressure
the Chinese president to "let my people go" — that is, to do something about the persecution of Christians and human rights abuses.

Most of the pressure on Clinton to be nice to the Chinese and
not to rock the boat is due to the fact that nobody wants to close
down the markets. We want to sell our goods to the Chinese. That
is all well and good, but it assumes that tyrannies can provide a
good economy. Classic examples of the kind of economy tyrannies

create are North Korea, Cuba, and the Soviet Union, which, after all, collapsed of its own weight.

Why do we insist on propping up the Chinese? Why do we look the other way when they torture people, kill babies, and burn churches? There may be a short-run gain in terms of a billion people buying our widgets (and not incidentally our being able to buy Happy Meal toys at McDonald's for a tenth of what they would cost if we were to produce them domestically), but in the long run it has to fail. The collapse of the Southeast Asian miracle economies is a perfect case in point.

What an amazing irony. The Chinese president comes to Washington with everybody salivating, all of the cash register mentalities clanging away, because we see this huge market, at the very same time that the rest of Asia is in shambles. Why is it in shambles? Because it missed Michael Novak's basic point.

Michael Novak, in *The Spirit of Democratic Capitalism*, says that free economies rest on a three-legged stool: political freedom, economic freedom, and moral consensus. The Chinese haven't got any one of the three, and they are woefully deficient on the third. So they are doomed. We are going to pump in all our money and foreign aid and watch the thing collapse anyway.

What the collapse in Southeast Asia shows us is that freedom and democracy are a prerequisite for a healthy, functioning economy. For us to continue to neglect human rights abuses is not only morally wrong—the issue is about what kind of people we are, not about our trade policies—it's also very shortsighted, because it does not lead China into freedom but into the model of other Asian economies, which are now up in smoke.

Even if we're not moved by moral concerns, we ought to be by pragmatic concerns. Doing business with the devil ends up being the devil's business.

# Are Christians Dangerous?

In recent years, Christians have borne the brunt of bias. Someone wrote that we were the last group in American life that could be discriminated against with impunity. I'm so sick of hearing people saying the new religious right is trying to impose its views on others, or Andrew Sullivan saying that we are the new Taliban.

We've taken a lot of heat over the years—we get called bigots and extremists and even accused of being homophobic and therefore responsible for the death of Matthew Shepard. So we're not strangers to this kind of stuff; it's been going on a long time. But there's a whole new wave coming, in my opinion, and it's going to be the most vicious ever—and also the most dangerous, because the form the attacks will take appeals to basic American instincts of fair play, and now particularly the American obsession for tolerance.

In the wake of September 11, we saw a lot of press comments attacking Christians for wanting to evangelize Muslims (or Jews, or Mormons) and for claiming that our faith is exclusive, meaning that you can only come into God's presence through Jesus.

I recently read an article by Steve Gushee, religion writer for the *Palm Beach Post*. I don't carry any water for Tim LaHaye, but when he gets attacked for defending the gospel, then I'm going to defend him. In this article, Gushee wrote that LaHaye's convictions about Christ are "inappropriate, ludicrous, and dangerous." And look at this phrase: "Contrary to most scholarly opinion, he [LaHaye] insists that the God of Islam is not the God of the Bible and that Muslims do not believe in the true God."[2]

Wow! Contrary to what scholarly opinion? Certainly not contrary to the Bible. Gushee also accused LaHaye of advocating the dangerous but popular opinion that Christianity is absolutely the only legitimate original religion in the world.

The *Bergen Record* said once that my comments were among the most dangerous that could be made anywhere in the world because I thought we should be converting Muslims.[3] I decided to ignore that article, but now I can't ignore it because it's part of a trend. I mean, you can see these things emerging. Here comes a cultural trend if I ever saw one, no question.

We will be attacked, as I was, at a luncheon in Silicon Valley with futurologist Paul Saffo, when I insisted that all religions are not alike. Supposedly when we make this claim, we are discriminating, we're being intolerant, we're being bigoted. My answer to Saffo, of course, was that I didn't insist on this; Jesus did, and if He expected me to be a Christian, I was going to believe what Jesus said.

Saffo kept demanding that I retreat from that position because he said he really believed all religions lead to the same place—they're all an attempt to find God, and they're all equal. He took great offense at what he called my "truth claim." But in the course of the argument I pointed out to him that, of course, he himself was making a truth claim: His truth claim was that all religions are equal, and my truth claim is that Christianity sets itself apart. I didn't even argue that it was right. I just said it sets itself apart as an exclusive truth. So do the other religions when you really study them; certainly Judaism does and Islam, stridently so. So I said, "Whose truth claim is correct, yours or mine? You say religions are all alike, and I say they are not because my Bible says they are not."

Then I argued they can't be all alike because the law of non-contradiction doesn't allow them all to be true at the same time.

So what the world is saying on its face is preposterous. It's not only discriminating against us, telling us we can't really believe what we believe; they're simply wrong about what the gospel says. This fellow Gushee was just in factual error, but you can see the pressure building.

The fact of the matter is what they're saying is all religions are alike and therefore we can't make any distinctive claim for Christianity. That in and of itself is a truth claim, which is flatly contradicted by the facts, unless you suspend the law of noncontradiction. The conclusions of the secularist are laughably preposterous, but this isn't going to stop them from making them, and this is the wave of the future persecution of Christians. But we need to be able to defend ourselves. The answer is to look at what the religions themselves say, the basic documents of the Bible, the Torah, and the Koran. Right there, you have three contradictive systems, all making truth claims.

I think Christians have to make this case very intelligently to people, and if we do, we'll be able to nip this thing in the bud.

Don't think I'm an alarmist; discrimination against Christian viewpoints is already happening in Denmark and in Canada. In Denmark Christian speech is called "verbal violence"; Canadians, too, are being restricted in what they say.

# Are We Tolerating Evil?

A recent front-page piece in the *New York Times* was headlined "More Christians Are Fleeing Iraq After New Violence."[4] This headline in and of itself is newsworthy. It's the first time that the *New York Times* has really acknowledged the problem. In fact, most of the media have ignored it. And the *Times* broadcasted it as the lead story in the paper. I give them credit for this.

The issue of Christians in Iraq hits home in a very powerful way. These Christians are descendants of the Chaldeans who were there right after the time of Christ. This is not some start-up religion, but it is a minority religion.

Now why is this happening? First of all, one would have to say the US government is allowing it, which is absolutely scandalous. If we threaten to cut off aid for the Iraqi government unless this is stopped, it would be stopped, or at least they would make honest efforts to stop it. And at least it would show that we're not going to tolerate it.

The second thing it shows, I'm sorry to say, is something even more ominous. I have come to believe that just under 20 percent of Muslims are disposed to violence and terrorism. A Gallup statistic in 2010 said 18 percent. And it's probably pretty close to the mark.

One thing we in the West should not do is equate all Muslims with the Islamists. Those who are not prone to terror and violence have every right to be treated just as decently and carefully as we would treat anyone created in the image of God. It's also counterproductive if we label the entire Muslim world with the Islamist stigma, because what that will do is produce the very clash of civilizations which the Islamists want, because they want to be at war with the West.

So I've come to applaud the efforts on the part of the US government to reach out to all peace-loving Muslims. After all, we believe in the words of the Declaration of Independence. "All men"—that's including Muslims—"are created equal and derive from their Creator certain inalienable rights."

Liberty, including religious liberty, being one of those rights. So when our men and women go into combat around the world, they are fighting not just for the rights of Christians, but also for Muslims, Sikhs, Confucianists—that is, all people. This is one of the unique things about the Western worldview. We care passionately for every single human being.

So our government is right to reach out lovingly to the Muslim world. We are right to defend the religious freedom of all human beings wherever they are. We are right to be tolerant of others.

But what happens when you are tolerant of others who are barbarically intolerant of other human beings? This is quite an interesting question. Are we tolerating evil when we tolerate those who perpetrate it?

I would say yes. This is the reason that what is happening in Iraq is so terrible, so egregious. We are parties to it on two counts: we're not condemning Islamists for it, but they are the ones responsible; and we're not using our own leverage supporting the Iraqi regime to stop it.

Tolerance is a wonderful thing when it is properly understood. In postmodern America we've distorted the meaning completely to say that everybody's point of view is equally valid. That's not true. The Islamist's point of view is not equally valid with the Christian point of view. We have to repeatedly make that case as we welcome peace-loving Muslims but denounce, and yes, fight against, if necessary, the Islamists. They're not responsible citizens; they're barbarians. And all civilized people should unite in opposition to them.

# 12

# SUFFERING

# The Paradox of Suffering

Malcolm Muggeridge once said, looking back on his eighty-odd years of life, that he realized everything he had learned had come as a result of suffering.

This has certainly been my experience. I wouldn't say *everything* I've learned came out of suffering, but suffering has certainly taught me the most important lessons. And I see in my life especially the incredible paradox of how God works.

Not long ago, Patty and I were staying in the Hilton Hotel in Ocala on our way back from a visit to the North Carolina mountains. When we came in that night, the doorman said that he wouldn't be there the next day, because something very important was going to take place: He was going to be baptized. We talked for a few minutes, and then I left with Patty to go to our room. But when I got to the elevator I had second thoughts. I realized I should go back and talk a little more with the doorman. So I did, and we had an absolutely wonderful conversation. We ended up praying together at the front door of the hotel.

When I finished praying for him, he had tears rolling down his cheeks. I also gave him a lot of good advice because he had the idea that all of his temptations, like his sins, would be washed away once he came out of the water. I explained to him that the Christian life is a growing process; you have good days and bad days. It was a really wonderful opportunity just to minister to the guy.

The next morning Patty and I were sitting at the breakfast table in the dining room when a gentleman came over with his son and sat down at the next table. He saw me and burst out—loud enough for most of the other people in the dining room to hear—"You're Chuck Colson! Mr. Colson, I just have to tell you that your book *Born Again* changed my life." The waitress overheard this and came over to the table. "You wrote *Born Again*!" she exclaimed, and began to explain what the book had done for her life.

It's amazing. I wrote that book decades ago, and everywhere

I go, I meet people whose lives have been impacted by it. I ended up having a wonderful conversation with the man in the dining room. He had quite a story; my book had driven him to C. S. Lewis, and he returned to the faith, which he had lost, got his life together, and is now a radiant Christian.

Patty and I talked a little bit about this, and it hit us both again: the most important things to come out of my life happened as a result of the Watergate disaster. We reminisced about what we went through: a reporter on the doorstep every morning, sensational headlines, absolutely outrageous charges, and some stuff that was just plain made up. My character was torn to pieces on the front pages of every paper in America. We endured this for two years, and then prison, and all that went with it. After twenty-five years, as we thought about it, it didn't seem so bad, but it was pretty horrendous at the time. We had no idea what the future would hold, or whether I could get a decent job or how we would support ourselves.

The first year out of prison wasn't a picnic, either. We had to put up with a lot of suspicion. Somebody threw a pie in my face, and somebody hit me at a Chicago airport. There was a total loss of privacy.

You look back on all of this and if you're a secularist—that is, if you believe there is no supernatural world—then this kind of suffering would seem unfair—a total waste, a negative, draining experience. It would leave you bitter—just the way most of the men coming out of Watergate were.

On the other hand, if you look into the spiritual realm and realize that there is a sovereign God, you see how He redeems suffering and how He, in fact, uses it for His purposes.

It's almost axiomatic. Christ had to suffer for us. Look at 1 Peter 4:1–6. It was Christ suffering for us that gave us freedom and deliverance from sin. It is our suffering in turn that God uses to redeem others.

Could He accomplish His will some other way? Sure. The fact of the matter is, His greatest work is done through defeats, brokenness, and suffering. It's one of the great mysteries of the gospel; it is the great central paradox.

It is also the suffering that has given meaning to my life, and given me fulfillment beyond anything imaginable.

# No Pain, No Gain

Christianity is frequently attacked by people who ask how a good, loving God permits suffering. But if we are to have free will—that is, a free choice about how we live our lives—then obviously, we're not always going to choose the right thing. So the fact of free will supposes there will be suffering, that there will be evil, that there will be wrong choices, bad decisions, and bad consequences.

You really can't have it both ways. If there were no suffering, no evil, no pain, no problems, it would be the result of the earth's entire population, always, without exception, choosing the right things. But if this actually happened, we wouldn't have a free moral will; we would be automatons. We would be puppets on a string, as C. S. Lewis argued.

The fact is that suffering, pain, and evil are the flip side of God caring so much about us that He gives us free wills. He did not create us as puppets. He created us as independent, free moral agents, able to choose right or wrong. But the flip side of that is that the world contains suffering and evil.

Interestingly, people really want to have it both ways. They criticize Christianity—how could God allow such horrors—and yet at the same time, they want to be free moral agents, and always have the right to be free moral agents, always making their own sacred choices regarding how to live. Sorry—you can't have it both ways.

Christianity is attacked for the fact that some of Christ's followers have done horrible things. Sadly, that's true, and no one should attempt to defend the indefensible. But when Christians do wrong, they're acting *against* what they believe, not in accordance with their beliefs. This is an absolutely critical distinction. Again, because we are free moral agents, we choose to do the wrong thing even though we know what is right, because Christianity teaches us the difference between right and wrong. We have to assume that knowing what is right sometimes is a restraint, and so even though Christ's followers sometimes do bad things, were they not Christians, they would behave even worse.

Remember Evelyn Waugh's argument, when he was confronted by a woman who told him, "Mr. Waugh, you say such horrible things to people, I cannot believe you are really religious. How can you behave as you do, and still remain a Christian?" Waugh replied, "Madam, I may be all the things you say. But believe me, were it not for my religion, I would scarcely be a human being."

The behavior of the believer has nothing to do with the truth of the belief system. It *should* influence how people behave, but it doesn't necessarily do this. Maybe, in fact, no one is really following what Jesus teaches, but that does not alter the fact that Jesus's teaching is true.

Again, we come back to the free will question, which is at the heart of our moral freedom and sense of responsibility. It is what makes us individuals created in the image of God.

# Calling to God in Agony

For thirty-five years I have been a Christian, and, I thought, pretty mature in my faith, teaching others, presenting myself as a leader, and always confident in my own abilities. But now I think maybe I did not learn the most important lesson of faith until this morning.

Last night, my daughter Emily phoned to tell me, somewhat sadly, that she had had a recurrence of the attack of the C-dif (Clostridium difficile). She tried to put a good face on it, saying it was not as bad as the relapses she's had before. On a scale of one to ten, it was somewhere between three and five. But it was devastating news for me, as it was for her, because she'd had a week of real progress, and she was just about to cut back to one pill a day in her doctor's effort to wean her off the Vancomycin completely.

I consulted everyone I know who has expertise in this area. They all said the same thing, which is what Massachusetts General Hospital said: this is the only drug that works. Sometimes in very stubborn cases it can go for a year or more. Most people get over it and then it comes back mysteriously or when they take an antibiotic. But the vast majority of cases are dealt with on one treatment or at most, two. Emily is now on her third extensive treatment, and the experts also told me that if this didn't work, they didn't have anything else except some drugs that are in final stages of trials with the FDA.

This is what one doctor calls a mystery bug. Others call it a superbug, which means that it is impervious to antibiotics.

I went to bed that night genuinely depressed. But as I lay there thinking, I decided that if someone is going to be a spiritual leader, he cannot succumb to fear. You have to have courage to believe, to rest in your faith, and if you feel weakness, at least never show it. So I resolved that I was going to trust God completely, that it was now beyond anything I could do, but I would not despair. I was able to get a decent night's sleep, though I hadn't expected I would.

When I woke up the next morning, some of the recent days' readings in *Streams in the Desert* kept coming to mind. Mrs. Cowman reminds us that we must pray believing, must trust God completely for the results, and must genuinely believe that the prayer will be answered and is answered.

This was not the name-it-and-claim-it gospel, obviously; no one writing for *Streams* would ever propose anything as ludicrous as that. God is not our celestial bellhop waiting for us to command Him to do things. Nevertheless, He's pretty strong about what we can do with real faith.

In one of the commentaries I read, it was said that Martin Luther took God's commands and his faith so seriously that when he was kneeling by his dying colleague Philipp Melanchthon, he "forbid death to take its victim."

In the *Streams* commentary that I reread the next morning, the writer said that God invites us to command Him to act. He further said: "What a distinction there is between this attitude and the hesitancy and uncertainty of our prayers of unbelief to which we have become accustomed. The constant repetition of our prayers has also caused them to lose their sharp, cutting edge."[1]

Thinking about these writings, I realized that my prayer time of half an hour to forty-five minutes at best, looking at my little green card with all the names on it, really had become a rote prayer. I think about the individuals; I hold them up before the Lord; I plead for them. But often I'm just going through the motions, and often it's kind of a hesitant, conditional prayer: "God, if you will see fit to do this" kind of thing.

Driven as I was this morning by my deep concern over Emily, I decided I didn't want to pray a superficial prayer. I dropped to my knees before the green library chair in my office and prayed intensely. I realized that if we're nothing but a product of fate, a chance collision of atoms; that if somehow through eons of evolution we have arrived at this sophisticated state where we have a conscience, where we feel emotions like love and care deeply about other people, where we have wonderful times to rejoice and times to weep and be sad; that if it all ends in death and there's no meaning to it—then nature has by its chance process pulled the ugliest imaginable hoax on humanity. It's impossible to imagine that nature could do this. And if it could do it, then there really is evil without good.

But we know there is good and evil. There's nothing more emphatically clear than that the entire dynamic of history and life is a battle between good and evil. It goes on constantly, between races, religions, nations and principalities, and in our own hearts. It goes on in the realm of the supernatural. This is the story of reality.

I also realized that *God is*, whether He ever answers my prayers, whether He takes my children from me or not. I can, with the hymn writer Horatio Spafford, sing, "It is well with my soul." Why? Not because I always like what has happened, but because I know God is the alpha and omega; He is the source of all reality. Without Him, we cannot explain our existence. He is.

These thoughts crowded into my mind as I was reaffirming my love for God and my desire to serve Him, and my recognition that He is omnipotent and that my life is in His hands. I exist only because He allows me to. There's no other explanation for my life, and for the things that have happened to me.

I remembered, too, that Jesus, when He prayed in Gethsemane, was sweating blood, which meant it had to have been an agonizing prayer, agonizing because He knew He was giving Himself up, and because He knew that He was taking all of the sins of all humanity upon Himself when He did so. He would have to have prayed with such intensity that blood seeped from His pores. I realized I'd never prayed with that kind of intensity. And so I tried to pray that hard.

Forty-five minutes later, I was thoroughly exhausted and drained. I stayed with this for almost an hour with an intensity I've not experienced before. I was prostrate before God, both literally and figuratively.

All the while I was praying, I could hear the fax machine going off, which really annoyed me. *Why can't people leave me alone when I'm praying?* I thought.

Getting up off my knees, I returned to my desk and continued praying and reading *Streams,* especially passages that seemed relevant to what I was going through. As I was reading and praying, another fax came through. Again, I was irritated. I finally went over to the fax machine and pulled out a pile of papers. The top one was from Emily, and it read: "Good news! I'm improving today! Prayer is stronger than flora! Yeah!"

The date stamp showed that Emily had sent it at 9:47 a.m. — fifteen minutes before I had finished praying.

Emily later told me that she had risen that morning surprised that she felt so good, because she expected to go through the same cycle she'd gone through before. And as she walked around, she began to feel even better, and she realized she had improved. She'd also received a good night's sleep, which didn't often happen when she got these attacks. And as she went through her morning routine, she began to feel even better. She debated telling me, and then finally decided, given that it was almost 10 a.m., it would be okay to interrupt me with a fax.

During my prayer time that morning, I had been bold enough to do a couple of things I haven't often done. I recognized that this superbug hit Emily at a time when she was just getting serious overtures from Zondervan to write a book about her autistic son, Max, which had the potential to be a blessing to so many people who have similar struggles.

Almost immediately after I told her about Zondervan's interest, she was diagnosed with an infected tooth, and then she had to have a root canal done. The dental surgeon gave her an overdose of the strongest antibiotic available, and the C-dif hit her that week. Coincidence? I don't believe so. I believe that these health problems were a direct attack by Satan to stop the work God wanted to do through Emily.

This war between good and evil goes on before our very eyes, and goes on in heavenly places. So yesterday, I commanded Satan to come out of Emily and to leave her alone, to depart. And I prayed in Jesus's name. I've always been more reserved than that, leaving that kind of thing to the charismatics. I then told the Lord that I believed He would answer the prayer in His good time.

But I also prayed, *Lord, what a wonderful thing it would be if you were to answer my prayer immediately.* And I prayed believing He would. Just minutes later, that fax arrived from Emily.

What's the real answer here? Faith is more than intellectual assent. It is a total surrender of one's self — something I've seldom exercised. I'm a control freak; I want to get God in on the act, but then I want to do my stuff.

No more. Of course, we should behave responsibly; of course we should get medical care when we need it. We all get sick at one time or another, and need doctors and medicine. But the most powerful thing that we can do is to totally put ourselves in God's hands and at His mercy.

I suspect that day changed my prayer life forever. I could never be satisfied again by rote prayers.

Emily and I later had one of the most wonderful telephone conversations ever in which she told me what had happened on her end, and I told her what had happened on mine. Then she said, "Daddy, we ought to pray about this." I led, and Emily prayed a very strong prayer after I finished.

I was in tears, listening. It was a wonderful moment between two Christians, a father and a daughter, who together knew beyond a shadow of a doubt that God is, that He is victorious in the battle against evil, and that He enlists us to be part of the work of His kingdom once we have total faith—faith without any qualification or reservation.

I realized after all this that writing that book was important, and was God's work, and that the enemy would use everything he had to stop it.

I've had experiences like this before while working on writing projects—I've had obstacles thrown in my way, endangering projects I thought God was really calling me to. But I'd never had an experience this intense.

I've seen God act. But I can't think of any experience I've had since I became a believer where a prayer was answered so dramatically—not, at least, since the prayer I prayed—"God, take me in"—in Tom Phillips's driveway, and He did. He answered that prayer immediately, and I've followed Christ ever since.

As I think back on it, it is because I didn't know any better, hadn't become sophisticated as a Christian, didn't understand the language or the habits or the disciplines. I simply called out in agony over my own sin that night, and asked God to take me just the way I was. It was total faith. I didn't doubt that He was there, listening to me, and I experienced a tremendous wave of relief, a surge of happiness and fulfillment and peace. God answered that prayer immediately, just as He did today, almost thirty-five years later.

Did the answered prayer mean all our problems are over, and that Emily will no longer have health issues or other obstacles? No. There will be setbacks for both of us. But at the end of the day, there is no question about the reality of God and the power He gives us through prayer and genuine faith. No one who experienced what I did this morning could ever doubt that.

We need to live lives that are totally trusting on Him and in His hands, knowing that the battle between good and evil goes on until Christ returns in His glory.

# Holy Abandon

Another quote from *Streams in the Desert*: "The capacity for knowing God enlarges when we are brought by Him into circumstances which obliged us to exercise our faith. So when difficulties beset our path, let us thank God that He is taking trouble with us, and lean hard upon on Him."[2]

This is precisely what Bob Rowling, the founder of TRT Holdings, said in a conversation with me, and I think it's a parable for what is happening in our culture today. People are going to become deadly earnest about their faith when they realize there are difficulties that they can do nothing to control. What's happening around us in culture is simply beyond any of us to fix. I hate to say it, but it looks as though it's beyond the ability of government to repair. So could God be putting us in a position where we have to depend on Him?

Trials and difficulties also make us confront the danger of anxiety, worrying, and fretting, which throughout Scripture we're told not to do. And it makes good sense that you wouldn't do it, because, as the very next *Streams* devotional said, "Worrying over what we have lost or what has been taken from us will not make things better but will only prevent us from improving what remains. We will only serve to make the rope around us tighter if we rebel against it."[3]

This is incredibly profound if you think about it. The harder you fight to get yourself out of something, the more you strain against the ropes that are around you, the more you hit your head against the wall in utter frustration, the deeper you fall into the hole. It's the time to lean back and really trust God, to really put your problems before Him. What this does, of course, is to not only lead to a solution; but the very act of doing it *is* the solution. Your faith is strengthened, and you've got some confidence about the future, without which you'll never accomplish anything.

People today are overwhelmed by anxiety. The people I talk to are really feeling it in terms of unemployment in their families, or the danger of seeing businesses lost, or philanthropic fortunes depleted. It's a really scary time.

This is precisely the situation in which Christians should do the very best of things. Because we do not let the circumstances control us, we do not succumb to anxiety. Anxiety leads to despair; despair is a sin because it denies the sovereignty of God. And how often do we have to keep repeating this? Fear is the enemy of faith; anxiety is the anti-God state. Despair is a surrender of faith.

How is this going to work out in a practical impact? If Christians really had this state of mind, if we really looked with total confidence to God, if we really lived lives of faith—reckless, holy abandon, if you will—would not the world see something really different in us, particularly when the world is cringing in fear, when so many people think everything is collapsing around them? In their fear, they would see us calmly, serenely, trusting in our Lord. And that's not some blind pacifism. That's faith. And if we live it out, think of the impact we'll have on people.

Circumstances are driving us to this. We either have to start helping our neighbors and doubling up on things, bringing the kids home, if necessary, from their newly unaffordable apartments and ensuring a place for them to live, or we're denying the reality of our faith.

# A Squadron of Angels

Michael Novak and I had a great conversation about death and suffering and love. It was a rich, one-hour conversation. The man is incredible. He should be preserved somehow, because there's so much in his mind.

One of the things he got me thinking about was how shallow the evangelical understanding of suffering is. There's a whole Catholic teaching on the theology of suffering, which, just going through a suffering experience as Patty and I had with her open-heart surgery, really hit home with me.

The other night Patty said to me that she was almost grateful that we'd gone through this. She said, of course, that we were already as close as two people could be, but it had strengthened our bond and commitment to each other. It had tested us. It had brought our family together in unexpected ways.

We saw real goodness in a lot of people. But here was the big reason Patty said she was glad we went through this. She said, "I feel like I have been drawn so much closer to God. I feel so much more of a personal relationship. I have seen Him work this week. I have experienced it, and there have been miracles."

She repeatedly talked about that. And for some reason I was drawn to repeatedly pray for a squadron of angels to surround us; and it has really happened. Not that there weren't setbacks. But we just sensed a calm about this that comes only from God.

If you believe we're just random collections of atoms and cells coming together in some odd pattern, well, what's the point of suffering, of death, of life?

I can tell you, this was a rich and meaningful experience, as exhausted as I am, and as weak as Patty is, and as fragile as we've discovered life to be. Jonathan Edwards was right: Life hangs by a thread. When you realize that someone is about to operate on your heart, and you realize that your life is on the line at that moment, it brings home the truth that should be uppermost in our minds all the time—that is, we dangle by a thread over the fires of hell. We have no claim on life, and no entitlement to live the next day or another week.

Here was one of the payoffs for me. This is classic Patty Colson wit. In the ICU there was a wonderful, beautiful Christian nurse. She just hovered over Patty. If I've ever seen an angel at work, it was this nurse. When Patty was coming out of the anesthesia, the nurse told her, "You're going to be better off now because you'll have a reengineered heart, a new heart." And Patty replied, "God already gave me a new heart before the operation." She said this with almost a twinkle in her eye.

When you see something like that, you realize what Catholics teach about the theology of suffering is absolutely so. It draws us closer to God in a way that nothing else can.

I went from a sense of shock when I found out Patty would need to have open-heart surgery to watching Patty get her courage up for the operation. It wasn't a conscious effort; she just got stronger and stronger. Then she really went through it with a great spirit. I don't think I heard her complain once. And this isn't just a testimony to Patty's character, though she's got a lot of it. It was a real testimony to God's grace. We experienced grace every step of the way, including the choice of a surgeon, who, I later found out, is considered one of the top heart surgeons in the country. He's a member of our church and we'd known him for years. He loves the Lord. He ministered to Patty during the whole process, including praying with her. We felt like God gave us that squadron of angels I asked for.

I saw something in the hospital and the rehab center that I had never before focused on. The nurses and the attendants get a kick out of seeing you get better. There was a little nurse named Jackie, a devout Catholic, who got so excited after the surgery. When Patty was able to take a couple of steps, she would clap her hands.

Yes, we live in a fallen world. But there's a good side to us, and our better natures come out in an experience like this. In the midst of all the evil and suffering and name-calling and stridency going on in our society, there are a lot of good people, just day in and day out, living their faith. It was a reaffirming experience for us, particularly in the cynical business I'm in of critiquing the false values of the culture and all that kind of stuff—a wonderful experience to see the good side of humans come out, and to see people's better nature going to work, and to see the helping hand that's extended to those who are sick and suffering and in need.

The effect on Patty and me is huge and will remain so. It probably wouldn't have happened but for the surgery.

# Mocked and Condemned

Kent Hill, the president of Eastern Nazarene College, was a colleague of mine in the Evangelicals and Catholics

Together (ECT) efforts. When he introduced me during one of the school's commencement exercises, he recalled an incident many years before when we, the evangelical leaders of ECT, were taking terrible public abuse. We were being called heretics and betrayers of the Reformation and other even less charitable characterizations.

During that time Prison Fellowship's contributions fell off substantially. We were able to document at least a million-dollar loss in support.

Kent told the crowd of an occasion following an ECT meeting in New York when we rode to LaGuardia Airport in the same cab. During the drive, we discussed the controversy that was affecting our ministries and reputations. When we got out at the airport, Kent told the students that before I said good-bye, I turned to him and said, "Kent, it doesn't matter. The controversy we have to endure. We are doing the right thing—and that's what counts."

Kent said that really gave him steel and also made him realize that these controversies do not reflect the real issue. The real issue is one of integrity.

# The Fellowship of Suffering

What does it mean to be Christlike? The apostle Paul says that he longed for the fellowship of suffering. Could it be that the Christian's purpose in the world is to share Christ's suffering, to bear the hurts and wounds of a world infected by sin—and to do this on the world's behalf? That is what would make us Christlike.

Christ took all the sins of the world upon Himself at one time—past, present, and future. But is it not part of being Christlike that we are taking sins and burdens and weights of the world upon ourselves on the world's behalf? The world won't appreciate this, or appreciate us, but nonetheless, that's our call.

What this means is that a meaningful life is a life in which we accept suffering—indeed, expect it—and somehow even rejoice in it, as hard as that is to contemplate. Think about Joni Eareckson Tada, who has gone through unbelievable suffering, and yet God has redeemed it all. It's almost as if she had to go through it to be able to speak for God at one of the most decisive moments in the great moral debate over what it means to be human.

# Persecution

**The peculiar reason I can write about persecuted** Christians and how our government should start cracking down is the fact that, as a going-away present from the White House, Nixon sent me on a mission to Russia. It wasn't just a going-away present; I was the one guy Nixon thought could tell the thugs then running the Soviet Union why the entire SALT negotiations in 1972 (by which we had agreed to a limitation on missiles in exchange for trade and the Russians being able to buy our grain) were going to go down the tubes because, while the Russians wouldn't believe it, Congress would torpedo our trade agreements if the Russians did not let out Soviet Jews.

So in February of 1973, I trotted off to the Soviet Union and negotiated for a week with Vasili Kuznetzof, who was the hardline deputy foreign minister, the tough guy they brought out to rebuff the West on everything. We had the Helsinki Accords going on, and negotiations in Geneva, and complicated stuff. I told Kuznetzof if they did not let out Soviet Jews that the Jackson-Vanick Amendment would pass in Congress and would cripple the trade agreement.

I was not there as a diplomat but as a politician telling him, "Here's the politics of Congress." We argued for a week, and he kept saying I was interfering in the internal affairs of the Soviet Union, and they didn't interfere in the internal affairs of the US. I said it wasn't a matter of internal affairs. Human rights are not granted by government but are transcendent; governments could neither grant them nor take them away.

On the day I was leaving we had a meeting in the afternoon—about twenty Americans on one side of the table, and twenty Russians on the other. Kuznetzof was shouting that I was interfering in internal affairs. I said, "Well, Mr. Minister, it will be your decision, because Congress will stop this trade. You will get no American grain."

I started to pack up my papers and he said, "You can tell your president we will do what is necessary because we respect the accords to the trade agreement in SALT."

He slammed down his papers, got up, and walked out mad. The next week they announced that thirty-five thousand Jews were being released from the Soviet Union.

So pressure does work. I know that if President Clinton and company were to put the screws on President Suharto of Indonesia, they would stop killing Christians in east Timor. They are massacring them.

Then you take the persecution of Christians in China; the house churches have been driven underground.

Look at the Middle East. It's just a travesty that we prop up these little tinhorn republics and they're persecuting Christians. I realize religious liberty is down the scale of national priorities these days, but it is shocking that the world's greatest military and economic power, which would send a half million troops halfway around the world to the Middle East to protect its oil supply in Kuwait, would not even express a whimper of outrage when they aren't allowed religious services at the American embassy in Saudi Arabia.

Why has America become a paper tiger? Because I think the Chinese have figured out that the buck is more important than anything else, and that we will do nothing to disrupt trade or inconvenience Americans who want to go into Radio Shack and buy a handheld calculator for $25, not $35, as I had to for a bigger, less efficient unit that sits on my desk, because every one of the handheld ones is made in China. No politician wants to upset the masses by telling them they can't get the products they want, the calculator being one of the dozens that, if you were to ban products from China, people could not buy a particular product of their choice. What greater American right do we want to protect than the right to buy any product we choose to buy?

The fact of the matter is that principled positions do result in good economic policies and good economic results, while unprincipled positions end up in failure. Unprincipled positions after World War I, with self-interest dominating the British, resulted in the horrors of World War II that would have been otherwise averted. So it may look like business is triumphing over human rights at the moment, but ultimately good human rights lead to good business.

# Outlawing Sin

I just read a piece in *Christianity Today*, "Brave New Salvation," that really impressed me.[4] It's way-out science fiction that's not so way-out. It presented the ultimate conclusion of the present biomedical craze at understanding, programming, and controlling the human genome. The article imagined what would happen if we could simply eliminate sin.

I also noticed an article in the *New York Times* titled "Six Billion Bits of Data About Me, Me, Me."[5] This was a particularly interesting piece because it really told us what we can currently do in the whole genome area. And good people like Francis Collins, the geneticist who headed up the Human Genome Project, love all this because they say that we'll find cures for all the dread diseases, and that we'll be able to make enormous advances in human civilization. And in one sense, he's right.

But the reason I'm less excited about it is that it's the ultimate in playing God. I can't argue that, if we could get rid of the defective genes that lead to things like Alzheimer's, that it would be a bad thing; in fact, I'd be the first in line to get my genes reprogrammed. Just think what an advance it would be if we could eliminate human suffering. Or would it?

All of our spiritual growth comes through suffering; there is no shortcut. Here, the Catholic theology is much better than evangelical theology. Catholics really mean it when they argue for adversity being a blessing.

What the human genome project doesn't take into account is the fallenness of human nature. This is why Agnieszka Tennant's piece in *Christianity Today* is so much on the money. The only way in which you could really enjoy all the advances of genetic engineering would be to eliminate sin. There has already been serious talk about finding the "crime gene" and knocking it out of people.

What we would then have accomplished, however, is the creation of a human utopia, totally humanly engineered. We would no longer need God. We would no longer need to have debates about whether God exists or doesn't exist. We would all simply live in absolutely restored Eden forever.

But just assuming there is a God, what do you suppose He's going to think of all this? His Son died on the cross so we could overcome evil. And now, in the test tube, we've found a way to eliminate it. We have just rendered Christ's sacrifice unnecessary. I'm not sure I can even think of all the implications of this.

These two articles posit a situation that raises ultimate theological questions. We are believers. We believe God created the universe, that He created us to live in a paradise. We blew it with our free will, and He redeemed us. Now we want to go back and rewrite human history and eliminate the fall. What does this tell us about ourselves, our relationship with God, the future, and the relevance of Christ?

# 13

# WAR of the WORLDVIEWS

## Where Does Religious Conviction Come From?

Do you remember the first time you heard the chicken and the egg question? Probably the original brain stumper to challenge kids to think, or to show them how tough some questions are, it has now become almost a cliché.

But that doesn't stop learned academics from spending vast amounts of time pondering such questions. One of the latest evidences of this is a book coauthored by Lionel Tiger, a professor of anthropology at Rutgers. The book is titled *God's Brain*.

Tiger reports that, according to statisticians, 80 percent of human beings have some religious identification. That's nearly five billion people. He then posits the question: Where did religious convictions come from? He didn't even give passing notice to the fact that these convictions might just come from the fact that there is a deity whom people are created to worship. No, his first suggestion was that religious belief systems depend more upon the "imaginative and deeply felt assertions of thinkers and advocates ... than on tough evidence."[1]

Oh? Well, at least he wasn't saying what Freud argued—that God is merely wish fulfillment, or what Richard Dawkins says, that we're actually deluded to think that there could be a God. Tiger instead argues that there is no supernatural; religious belief is only a natural phenomenon.

The reason he said this is that, in his view, religion is a product of neuropsychological engagement. He acknowledges this is a drastic view of Darwinism, and a decisive disproof of human, godly origins. In other words, there is no supernatural, only natural; science has discovered a part of the brain that processes moral decisions.

Tiger goes on to explain a number of so-called connections between social behavior and brain chemistry, including the secretion of the neurotransmitter serotonin, and the sense of status each individual possesses.

We have, according to Tiger, evolved in such a way that the brain actually makes us think that we really want God, that we are indeed now genetically disposed to take on the belief system of the social group we're part of.

This is all interesting speculation. I have followed developments in this field rather carefully, because in my opinion they do nothing but validate what the Bible already teaches.

The problem with Tiger's assertions is that the brain never would have evolved that way if natural selection is right, if the survival of the fittest is true. The whole pattern of evolving moral consciousness would be survival. That would be the ultimate good, the ultimate consequence of the brain adapting or evolving over the centuries to follow self-interest. So even if we were to acknowledge, for the sake of argument, that the brain might have evolved, it wouldn't have evolved the way it did, driving us to care about others and be willing to lay down our life for them.

In this vein—if our brains are a product of evolution, with all this moral processing in our brains—then no one would ever choose the God of the Bible. I doubt they would choose Allah, either. Why would you want to invent, by natural phenomenon, a god who demands that you give your life for another? That's what Jesus did. That's the whole essence of the gospel. And we see evidences of this motivation in the Old Testament. When I read Tiger's article, I was just studying the passage in Scripture where Joseph puts his brothers to the test. Clearly, he was trying to find out if they were willing to give up their lives for another. In Islam you give up your life for Allah. That's not a god you'd want to invent, nor is that a natural consequence of survival being wired into you as the ultimate moral virtue. Quite the contrary.

The apostle Paul told us that even in the case of Gentiles who had never heard of the biblical law, the law is actually written on their hearts. What modern science is telling us is that, indeed, the law is written on our hearts. But what evidence is there that this came about by evolution, since we know from the beginning of recorded human history that mankind has experienced a genuine, deep, and almost universal longing for God?

There you have it: the chicken and the egg. Which came first? Something in the natural process that gave us a desire for God then created a demonstrable need for God? The brain, as scientific studies are increasingly showing us, actually is, as the apostle Paul said, wired for God. But did that happen as a result of some natural process? Or did that happen because God made us, wired us, in fact, to want to seek Him?

Tiger said, "The stunning possibility is that religion will find its sturdiest roots in the natural, not the supernatural."[2]

Okay, the chicken came before the egg, but who made the chicken? To think that learned scholars can spend vast amounts of time contemplating such questions is bewildering. Particularly when I believe, as I do and have frequently said, that the presupposition "God is" is far more rational than the presupposition "God isn't."

When you compare how the consequences of the proposition "God is" lead to far more livable conclusions than the proposition "God isn't," when you look at the history of Western civilization and the impact of the Judeo-Christian tradition on the growth of that civilization, a very strong case can be made that "God is" is the only rational conclusion. It is the only one that provides a system that people can live with.

I've written about this at length, and have posted articles about this and charts that show how to compare the different worldviews. I've never read anything that counters this, nor have I been challenged in making this argument.[3]

Somewhere Cornelius Van Til wrote that " 'God is' is the only rational proposition." He further argues that he could show all other propositions irrational. He was right. And that is the best test of truth. Does it conform to the way things really are?

# The Death of Truth

A new, aggressive breed of atheists is out there, hawking books, shouting from the rooftops, and really asserting a proposition that not only is there no God, but also that if there were, He'd be evil, along with religion itself.

This is new. The old guard humanists are beginning to question this, as rightly they should. These are the folks who wrote *The Humanist Manifesto.* They're really not bad people; they just don't believe in God. But they do believe in helping other human beings. The old guard is saying, "Why can't we advance humanism by working hand-in-hand with people who believe in God?"

But the neo-atheists want nothing but our total elimination—unconditional surrender. Dawkins, Dennett, Hitchens all want to wipe religion off the face of the earth because, according to them, religion is a poison, a toxin—something that breeds fascism.[4]

Atheists used to be gentlemen because they were really trying to accomplish something good. The new atheists are on a search-and-destroy mission.

The old guard had their own belief system, and if we wanted our belief system, that was okay. The new breed reflects the death of truth. If there is no truth, then you can't really tolerate someone who says there is a truth claim, particularly if it's a truth claim that may in some way impinge upon your freedoms. So the new left—and that's what they are—aren't content with peaceful coexistence. They demand the elimination of the traditionalists. The reason is, we stand in the way of their worldview.

The new atheists are exactly like the communist dictators who feared religion more than anything else because it was a competing truth claim. And they would not tolerate anybody who worshiped any other god than Caesar (which takes us right back to New Testament times). The Star of David and the cross of Christ have been a scandal throughout history to every totalitarian leader who encountered them.

In my view, the new breed of atheists is totalitarian. They want total control for their worldview, which says there is no truth. What happens if they can enforce this?

There's an important nuance here. I can disagree with people without wanting to wipe them out. If I were to want to wipe out those I disagree with, the only reason I would do so is because they become such a threat to my truth claim. But of course, I would never do that. If you believe that truth will win out in the end, then you have no problem with having others make their claims without feeling they have to be destroyed.

# Poor Bill Gates

I just read an article about Bill Gates and his charitable endeavors that I find absolutely fascinating. The writer, Robert Barro, came to a number of the same conclusions I did, that Gates is going to go crazy trying to give that much money away when most of Africa lacks infrastructure, so you can't get the money into the hands of the people.[5]

But he also picked up another very interesting point. Gates assumes that he has to sell all his corporate stock, put it into his foundation, and give it away in order to do something worthwhile with his life. He told the Harvard graduating class that he hadn't realized when he himself was a student at Harvard how much disparity there was in wealth in the world. Now that he knows it, he wants to go on this great crusade to give all his money away.

Barro made the important point that what Gates has already done in building Microsoft and providing jobs, etc., is probably contributing more to the overall wealth in the world than anything he can do by bouncing all over Africa handing out packets of money. In fact, as Barro whimsically put it, he could do better by giving every man, woman, and child in America a check for $300. That's a little extreme.

But what Barro misses is that work and vocation are callings of God. If Bill Gates didn't live in that rarefied atmosphere of Seattle on the left coast and instead had a little understanding of the Christian view of both theology and history, he would see that the development of the work ethic is a distinctly Christian contribution. He would see that most of the great innovations that provided jobs and indeed the rise of capitalism itself was a Christian contribution.

Poor Bill Gates, he has all this money and a guilt complex. He talked about his guilt complex in his address at Harvard. He apparently sees everything he's done up until now as mere preparation for remedying the plight of the world's poor.

This is an admirable notion, but totally utopian, and misses completely what the meaning of work and wealth production and vocation really are.

There's nothing wrong with Bill Gates giving away his money to the poor; it's admirable, and I hope he succeeds. He faces an uphill struggle, however, to get that money distributed to people really in need. Bono and Bob Geldof and all these guys have been trying to do this for years with all of their concerts and pleadings and urgings of the G8, and what have you. All they've succeeded in doing is pumping more money into a system that ends up in the Swiss bank accounts of African dictators.

I really feel sorry for Gates, even as I applaud his philanthropic desires and his compassion for the poor. I share that compassion, having worked in prisons all these years and realizing how many people in the world never get a break.

But there's no reason for a guilt trip. No matter how much good he does with all this money he's going to give away, it will never do as much good as he did in creating innovations that have connected the world. Just think what the Internet means to people in remote regions. Think how it has sped up our communications as a nation, and what it has done for the development of business and industries.

In the Christian concept of vocation, this is Bill Gates's contribution. Luther said it doesn't matter whether you're preaching the gospel or cleaning the floors, as long as you're doing it to the glory of God. In the Reformation, the first act of discipleship was finding a vocation.

What a shame so many people go through life as Bill Gates

does, doing great things, not realizing their significance, and then finally arriving at a point where they think, "Now I can stop all that and really start doing something worthwhile." In the case of Gates, he may never do anything as worthwhile as what he's already done. But he can't appreciate that unless he has a Christian understanding of the view of life and the importance of work, and the way in which the dignity of work contributes to the well-being of others. If he did, he wouldn't have to go running around Africa trying to drop off bags of money. And he wouldn't have to repent of his past.

# The Fight of Our Lives

In my more reflective moments, I think about my own life experiences and where I found the greatest fulfillment and contentment. Interestingly enough, it was in the Marines.

Maybe these are the frustrated ramblings of an old man. But the thing that has distressed me most about the church is that we don't have the sense of loyalty and commitment to one another that I experienced in the Marines.

For me, it was politics that made me feel I was living in the jungle. It was dog-eat-dog, a battlefield all day, with people pitted against each other. I had become so exhausted by it that when I was welcomed into The Fellowship by Doug Coe, I thought I had arrived in heaven, just to be away from that and to really be able to trust people.

I realize now, as I look back on it, what I was longing for was that same sense of trust I had in the Marines. My platoon sergeant would have taken a bullet for me, and I think I would have for him. And of course, Al Quie turned out to be a guy who was prepared to take a bullet for me in the Christian faith.

As I say, maybe I'm getting older, I'm getting jaundiced, but I don't see that same mutual commitment to support one another in the Christian faith. It just isn't there. Everybody's got his own little territory he's protecting; there isn't the wholesale giving of ourselves to one another.

This really has been working on my mind as I've been writing the book with Emily about Max. Max has taught us how to love. Special needs kids are a gift to the world because they teach us sacrificial love. I also have realized, drawing on the Marine Corps analogy again, that this is the way Marines think about their platoon. They're willing to give their lives for their brothers.

I don't see that in the Christian world. I see people quarreling and quibbling with one another. I see us with a rear-echelon mentality most of the time. I don't see cooperating and pulling together.

This is what motivated my desire to convene a movement and get people working together across the divisions. It fueled my desire for Evangelicals and Catholics Together. I really think, if we take seriously God's commands to us, we're willing to lay our lives down for each other because that's what He tells us to do. But most of the time we're fighting each other and quibbling.

What put this into focus for me was reading a book called *Joker One*, written by a Christian by the name of Donovan Campbell, who graduated from Princeton and then went into the Marines. There's no worldview angle to the book, but it is a gripping, riveting read. I'd say it's one of the most engaging books I've read in several years.

I could really relate to it, even though I never got into combat and Campbell was in the worst of the battles in Ramadi, Iraq. But I could relate to it because the dynamics of building the relationships within a Marine Corps platoon are the same, whether you're being shot at or not. I was in a banana revolution, so to speak, in Central America, and thought I was going to be shot at. So you prepare for it. You're thinking about it all the time.

All the time I went through basic training I was thinking about the fact that I was going to have the lives of fifty men in my hands, and it weighed on me heavily. It matured me in a hurry, taking a carefree college kid who was having a lot of fun at parties and turning me into a man, because I knew I was going to be responsible for the lives of other people.

What brings all this into focus is Campbell's analysis near the end of the book. Why did these men go through all these firefights and battles and patrols and casualties, people being killed protecting one another, and caring most for the safety of their men — why did they go through all this? Was it love of country? Was it love of the Corps? And Campbell concludes that what really holds a Marine platoon together is love. There's an amazing chapter in his book describing this. When I read it, I identified immediately, because there was not a man in my platoon that I did not love. I must say, I did get very high marks from the people in our platoon, because they knew I loved them. And I think we would have died for one another in combat.

I think, if I had to diagnose the condition of the evangelical world, it is that we have a peacetime mentality. But we are at war; we're at war with Satan; we're at war with a world that is hostile and angry with us. We're fighting for our very lives. And yet, we have a rearguard mentality. We have a peacetime mentality. We can't afford the luxury of quibbling with each other instead of really pulling together.

I can only conclude from all of this that we don't really believe what we read; we don't really believe we're in a fight for our lives, and as a result, we don't have this kind of commitment. If we were in a physical war, we'd be taking bullets for one another. But here we are in a spiritual war, and we're fighting over music programs and other things that don't matter. Ninety percent of the stuff I have to contend with doesn't matter.

If we really understood what we're up against, we wouldn't look anything like we look. I don't write this to discourage people. But I don't know what it's going to take. We've somehow got to help Christians understand that we're really in the fight of our lives. We don't have time to be quibbling with each other. Look how Jesus treated His disciples when they were wondering who was going to be sitting next to Him in heaven. What is wrong with us?

I would recommend Campbell's book to anybody because, first of all, it's a great story, and second, it's one of the best love stories I've read. And love is the ultimate goal of our faith.

# Hoist on Their Own Petard

The debate continues over global warming. No one really knows for sure what causes it. But one thing is clear: We ought to be conserving energy. And as Christians we ought to be in the vanguard of care for the creation.

At times the debate has seemed unfortunately divisive. Some Christians do not think the Kyoto Treaty is the answer. (Nor does the US government at this point.) Some people aren't convinced that we are taking the right measures to deal with global warming. Some very respectable voices have been raised in the evangelical and conservative Catholic communities cautioning against the excesses of the environmental movement.

I quite happily signed a document prepared by the National Association of Evangelicals. This document, *Loving the Least of These*, listed the major priorities of the evangelical movement and identified creation care as one of our responsibilities.

But the debate has become divisive. The press has enjoyed exploiting differences on this issue between conservative Christians and liberal Christians. One group put together a document called the "Evangelical Climate Initiative" and ran a full-page ad in the *New York Times*. Those of us who are regarded as conservatives weren't even asked to sign it; I can only assume, based on other articles the *Times* has run, that its editors wanted to sggest that the evangelical ranks were split over environmental issues.

This is pure nonsense, as I have said many times. We are all concerned with finding the right means for protecting the environment.

Controversies like this are painful, particularly when the press thinks it can exploit differences in evangelical ranks. But I've discovered a hidden blessing in all of this debate. It is simply assumed today because of this debate that Christians ought to care about the environment. Thirty years ago, nobody would have made that assumption—because nobody saw biblical Christianity as a worldview. They saw it as an isolated separatist movement, concerned only with personal salvation.

What has happened as a result of this debate is to reaffirm the fact that Bible-believing Christians do have a worldview; faith does affect all of life. Christianity is not just about our personal salvation. Christian worldview deals with the workplace, the neighborhood, politics, arts, science, literature, music, and the environment. And the more the environmentalists beat us over the head for not doing enough, the more they are making the case that we Christians do have a biblical worldview.

Carry this another step further and you could say the critics of Christianity tell us we should keep our faith private: Don't get involved in abortion politics, don't get involved in any political debates. Don't impose your views; just stay out of people's way. But these same critics are demanding we do more about the environment.

There's a real inconsistency there. If we ought to be concerned about the environment, we ought to be concerned about the unborn in the womb, and the human rights of people around the world. And of course what happens in politics makes a big difference in terms of the social justice agenda that Christians pursue.

I love to hoist people on their own petard.

# Human Absurdity

Malcolm Muggeridge once quipped that since there were no bounds on human absurdity—the human condition never changes—there will always be humor. He said this when he was taking over the editorship of *Punch* magazine. The absurdity of humans knows no limits.

That's being demonstrated again in a new intellectual fad sweeping college campuses and bursting into public discourse. The idea is simply this: humans have been around a long time; they've had the capacity to make tools; Neanderthals had brains, and so on. So what makes things different now? Why is there this sudden explosion of knowledge and progress?

The answer is that we've developed a "collective brain." This proposition was posed in a major article in the *Wall Street Journal*. The question was asked, Why has culture exploded? Matt Ridley, writing in the *Journal*, said, "The answer lies in a new idea, borrowed from economics, known as collective intelligence: the notion that what determines the inventiveness and rate of cultural change of a population is the amount of interaction between individuals."[6] Suddenly we have this collective awareness, which has led to human consciousness. He called it "the big bang of human consciousness" that scientists have been looking for in the brain or genetic system, but they've been looking in the wrong place. It is simply the collective wisdom of people finally trading or bartering back and forth.

Now, you can postulate something like this and make a perfectly presentable case. The trouble is, history completely refutes it. We have only to look at history from the beginning of recorded evidences of it to see that people developed very sophisticated civilizations before the advent of Christianity.

Certainly the Greeks did. So did the Egyptians and the Romans. Evidence of ancient civilizations goes way back. And there was an amazing sophistication to them. I visited Pompeii and saw the ruins of that city. It is an extraordinary sight, to think of how sophisticated the Romans were in many respects.

But the turning point in history, the "big bang" that everybody is looking for, came with the Jews and the Christians, who burst onto the Greco-Roman Empire with a very radical idea: the revelation that God created us in His image, which sparked a whole different understanding of who we are. It was a revolution.

The Greco-Roman Empire, like most empires before it, had a caste system. Philosopher kings reigned and slaves worked. The whole idea stifled creativity. Slaves would always be slaves, and a ruling class would always tell them what to do.

If you read Rodney Stark's *The Victory of Reason*, you will understand fully why the course of humanity has changed so radically and dramatically in the last two thousand years.[7] You will understand the explosion of creativity, the big bang of human consciousness. It was this central idea that a sovereign God had created us in His image, had given us free will, had given us creative gifts, and our task was to use them for His glory. That revolutionary idea built Western civilization. It gave us the gift of reason. It enabled us to use the logical principles and rhetorical teaching we'd received from the Greeks for the ultimate good of all human beings.

This was the revolution that scientists are looking for.

When our kids come home from college and say they've discovered how collective cultural activities (a catchy euphemism for having sex with each other) created the great civilization we now have, you can tell them there is absolutely no historical, biological, or archeological evidence to support that proposition. To the contrary, when they study the history of Christianity—oh, if I could just get more Christians to study their own history—they will see that Christianity built the West, saved the West, delivered humanity, and gave us the explosion of ideas and creativity that is still so dramatically changing the world.

## Christians versus Pagans

I recently read a dynamite article titled "Our Religious Destiny," written by Arthur Brooks, a respected secular scholar who has written some great stuff, particularly about Christians being more charitable.[8]

Brooks says that conservatives are going to win the culture war simply because of the demographics. The same thing happened in ancient Rome; Christians—who took seriously the biblical command to be fruitful and multiply—had babies and the pagans did not. Too many babies were being killed when they were born. Rodney Stark writes about this in *The Rise of Christianity*.[9] The Greco-Roman world had a low view of marriage, and they couldn't induce people to have children. But Christians condemned promiscuity, which meant that sex remained within marriage, which meant that fertility was higher. Stark has all the statistics and makes a very compelling case.

What happened in ancient times is a perfect parallel with today. The low fertility rate meant that the ancients had to have higher immigration to get the work done (sound familiar?).

Eventually they lost the cohesiveness of their culture and the ability to defend themselves. So Rome fell.

What survived was the Christian church, because it had been multiplying. And what is going to cause Christianity to recover in the West is precisely the same phenomenon.

Brooks nailed it. This is a tremendous point. It's one of hopefulness and encouragement, demonstrating that when Christians live out the biblical worldview, we become the source of renewal in culture.

A lot of people think the West is in irreversible decline. But Arthur Brooks gives us reason to believe it isn't. Why? Secularists are declining in number because of their lower birth rate. Christians who are taking the biblical command seriously to be fruitful and multiply have a much higher replacement rate. So what's going to happen? Serious Christians soon are going to outnumber decadent pagans.

It happened in Rome. It's happening again.

# The Human Mosaic

When I was at King's College in New York—a great time, by the way—during the question-and-answer period a student asked me, "Since we believe that all human beings are equal, all created in the image of God, is it not a Christian duty to see that all people get equal benefits in a society?"

This is a question I've heard often, and I gave it the best answer I could. But I'm not sure I couldn't have done it better.

We talk about equal rights and equal human dignity. Our founders said, "We hold that all men are created equal." My answer to the student's question is that we are all created equal in terms of human dignity, not in terms of physical characteristics, abilities, intellect, and certainly not the results we achieve in life. Albert Einstein had a greater brain than anyone else in his era, and of course he achieved great things. So nobody can realistically expect that all people are created equal in terms of the characteristics and capabilities they're endowed with. Some people are born tall with great athletic ability; some people have no athletic ability but they have a wonderful spirit to encourage others. The human race is really a mosaic of all these talents and gifts being used, out of which comes a functioning community.

Nobody is guaranteed they'll be six feet tall and handsome with an IQ of 180. What the Christian doctrine teaches is that we are all invested with equal dignity. My grandson Max, who has trouble communicating, has the same human dignity that President Obama has, or some of the great minds of the day.

# Defying the Evidence

It never ceases to amaze me that people are willing to bet their lives on naturalism; not only is it self-refuting, but to believe it is an act of supreme hubris.

I say supreme hubris because naturalism is the assumption that the only thing that can be known is that which you see and can validate with one of your five senses. So what the naturalist is really saying is, if I can't prove it's true, then it can't be true. If I can't, by physical observation, conclude something is real, then it *can't* be real.

Of course, there are all kinds of things in life that we cannot see or apprehend with our senses that are nonetheless true, love being one of the most obvious. The principle that allows an airplane to fly, the lift created by air traveling more slowly under the wings than the air over the wings, is a visible principle, but you can't see the air actually moving. It is measurable, of course, but still a certain amount of faith is involved in knowing anything.

The naturalist, of course, says he can empirically validate this. He can see the airplane flying, and he can measure the speed of air over the wing so he can prove that it is true, or he can see someone making a sacrificial gesture on behalf of someone else, which is how we would define love. That's quite true. You can see the consequences of things which aren't knowable by the senses. And this, of course, is the very point that we seek to make. Let's look at how things work. Truth, after all, is the way things are. It's reality, so let's try different ways to live and let's see how they work out.

Over a period of time you can quite easily measure the consequences of certain moral actions and they are consistent. In all times and places you will invariably get certain consequences from certain moral behavior. If you look at it broadly enough, it's like an airplane wing. You're going to be able to see that the airplane takes off every time it reaches a certain speed. You're going to also be able to see that every time certain behavior takes place there are certain predictable consequences.

As C. S. Lewis argued so eloquently, naturalism is basically self-refuting because the assumption, the operative presupposition, is that everything came to be as a result of chance. Atoms merged at a certain point, there were chance mutations, perhaps in an infinite universe, and here we have these incredibly sophisticated humans who can develop incredibly sophisticated computers, and so on.

However, to come to that conclusion, you're relying on a brain and a thinking process that evolved by chance. If it has evolved by chance, you have no idea whether it's reliable. Attempt to prove to me that an organ that evolved by chance is going to be reliable to always give you the right answer to any particular question. Or prove to me that this organ has the capacity of knowledge, which is distinguishing what is real from what isn't. The answer, of course, is that you can never get there.

The naturalist is proceeding in blind faith. He is defying what is self-evident, both in nature and the creation and in terms of our moral inclination. He is, as Lewis said, like a man trying to lift himself up by grabbing himself by the collar and raising his hands. He won't get off the ground, but he will very likely strangle himself.

The naturalist is in the position of assuming that he knows everything he needs to know, and that everything that can be known is accessible to him through his senses. It takes an extraordinary leap of faith to arrive at that conclusion. But once you do, you have nothing. You are defying the evidence.

# Where Virtue Thrives

Courage, also called fortitude, is the first virtue, I believe, because without courage you can't follow your convictions on the other virtues.

Justice has to be one of the highest goods that people try to seek in society. Remember, Plato wrote his book *The Republic* to answer the question; What is justice? I'm not sure he actually answered it. I've done lectures on this subject, saying that justice is giving each one his due (that's the secular version), and that leads to distributive and retributive justice. But justice is also *shalom*, conditions for human flourishing—at least, in the Christian view. This is why Prison Fellowship worked with President George W. Bush to try to end prison rape.

Prudence is a wonderful virtue because we have to know when and how to speak; it's really a result of wisdom, of really seeking wisdom. We know how to speak with friends, we know how to deal with problems.

Prudence doesn't mean that you don't take strong action. It doesn't mean that you just moderate everything. It doesn't mean what Aristotle meant with "the golden mean." It means that you are wise about what you do, judicious. You balance things out. Of course, you make prudential arguments in the public square; you use a biblical framework for the argument, but you argue prudentially about what is good for the general welfare. And that may be the bottom line. Prudence really is working for the common good and doing what benefits the most people.

Temperance is about moderation in habits, which has to do with how we dress (not provocatively, for example). It's our speech: do we restrain that wicked instrument, the tongue, that the apostle James talks about? And consider alcohol. I was once a heavy social drinker, but not an alcoholic. But I have seen the ravages that alcohol has inflicted on people. I don't believe it is wrong to drink; nothing in the Bible says so. But maybe it isn't the best behavior for some of us. I've always been impressed with George W. Bush's statement that he always thought he could take ten drinks or one. But when Laura asked him if he could remember the last day he hadn't had a drink, and he couldn't remember, he decided that it was time to quit.

We've seen alcohol abuse in the prisons; we've seen the abuse of drugs, which are even worse, like crack. I used to be a heavy smoker, and I think it's harder to shake nicotine than anything else.

Humility comes with prudence. I think it was Socrates who was asked, "Who is the smartest man in the world?" He replied, "I am." "How do you know?" his interrogator asked. "Because I know I don't know everything," Socrates answered.

The virtue of faith is wired into every human being. All the studies show that people are irresistibly religious. They are looking for the transcendent, and spend most of their lives trying to figure out what it is that is above them, and where they come from. Whatever you call it—meditation, yoga, any of the things New Agers do, or any of the things that the Eastern religions teach—they're always looking for the transcendent, nirvana. So man is irresistibly or incorrigibly religious, someone once said.

No matter what conclusion we come to about God, religion is still wired into us. Richard Dawkins could not quite deny the possibility that there is a God. No one can look at creation and really deny it. As we read in Romans 1:20: "For since the creation of the world God's invisible qualities—his eternal power and divine nature—have been clearly seen, being understood from what has been made, so that people are without excuse."

Now, the secularist says, "You're relying on faith; I'm relying on science." Hah! What the secularist does is have faith that certain presuppositions, which secular scientists embrace, are true. He has to believe that we arose from a primordial soup, and any evidence that we didn't rebuts his case.

As T. M. Moore, dean of the Centurions Program, likes to argue, faith has to precede anything, because everybody has to have faith in some proposition that begins to explain things. C. S. Lewis noted that what debunks materialism is the fact that, if there is a blind natural process, then your brain, which gives you these conclusions, is the result of blind chance, natural process. So how can you trust it, if there is no faith, no basis for faith in anything?

What Christians mean by faith is simply that we trust. I trust the proposition "God is." I also happen to believe it's the most rational proposition, and I trust the historical data that supports the resurrection and the historicity of the Scriptures. So my faith is pretty firmly rooted in a rational basis. I think secularists are irrational. They claim we are, that we're relying on magic or unseen, invisible things, and religion is all a hoax put on to placate the masses. Quite the contrary. There is far more evidence that our faith is well-grounded than that their faith is well-grounded.

The virtue of hope is neat: Everybody needs hope in their lives. If their circumstances are tough, they have to hope they're going to get better. Hope is that which you seek, and the belief that what you seek can be realized.

I think about myself as a kid growing up. My dad had worked his way through both law school and accounting at night. He never really had a college education. I had every hope and expectation of being able to attend college, which I did, with a scholarship. Later, I had the hope that I would get into politics and make a difference, and I did, although not all for the good. But I've always had something in my life that I hope for. And even at this age, and having just had an accident that easily could have taken my life, my hope is in Christ.

I think it has to be said that fear, which is the enemy of faith, also denies us hope. Most of us expect the worst most of the time.

But the Christian has the great eschatological expectation—the return of Christ and the bodily resurrection and His reign. That is a wonderful hope. Show me somebody who can live without hope, and I'll show you a suicide waiting to happen.

But what kind of hope can the nonbeliever have? That he's going to live forever? No, he knows better. Perhaps he hopes he's going to live long enough to see his great-grandchildren, or that he's going to spend the rest of his days playing golf, chasing that silly little white ball over the grass, counting the number of days he may have left to play before he dies.

When I was in the hospital in 1987 having a tumor and 60 percent of my stomach removed, a staph infection set in. The nurses called my family in late one night because they really thought I wasn't going to make it. In between my spells of delirium, I was thinking, *Well, if I die, I'll be with the Lord. How does somebody who doesn't know the Lord endure this?* And that hope, the expectation of Christ and His return, sustained me through those incredibly agonizing and dangerous twenty-eight days. I've been thinking a lot about that recently in the light of the dangerous fall that I took. I realize God spared me, and there was a purpose in it.

The virtue of charity is a big one, and here is where the world gets it all wrong. The world sees nothing but erotic love, or self-seeking love. There are four kinds of love—*storge, eros, phileo,* and *agape.* What Christ is talking about throughout Scripture is God's love, which is *agape,* that allows us to do things that we would never, left to our own devices, do. It's unimaginable to me that Al Quie could have offered to serve my prison sentence if he was not experiencing something close to God's love. I feel the same way about Emily, as I wrote in her book, *Dancing with Max.* To watch her give herself totally and selflessly to her son has been really inspiring and a real example of *agape* love.

I don't know that I've ever shown *agape* love in my own life. I've said that I would lay my own life down for my brothers, but would I? I've never really been put to the test, so how do I know? Most people go through life not realizing it, but when they hear this little ditty about how the greatest of these is love, they immediately think of family and friends and romances. That's not what God is talking about. He's talking about dying to yourself and living for others; loving your neighbor more than you love yourself. "Greater love has no one than this: to lay down one's life for one's friends" (John 15:13). That's what He was talking about, the kind of love that Jesus showed on the cross.

# Breaking the Spiral of Silence

*On March 30, 2012, Chuck was giving the following speech when, according to Prison Fellowship employee Martha Anderson, Chuck "had to keep pausing to collect his thoughts." He eventually collapsed midsentence. Two staffers caught him and helped him to a chair, where Chuck attempted to continue his speech. But it was clear that something was very wrong. An ambulance was summoned, and Chuck was loaded onto a stretcher and taken to a hospital. He'd had a stroke.*

*"It's really remarkable his thoughts were as lucid as they were given what must have been going on inside his body and brain at the time," Martha says.*

*Chuck underwent surgery for an intracerebral hemorrhage at Fairfax Hospital in Virginia, and spent the next three weeks there. He went to be with the Lord on April 21, 2012, at the age of eighty, his family at his side.*

*On Friday, April 27, Chuck was buried with full military honors at Quantico National Cemetery. On May 16, 2012, thousands of mourners — from US senators to former prison inmates — attended a memorial service for Chuck at the National Cathedral in Washington, DC.*

*In this, his last speech, Chuck gives a final warning: Our culture is at a crossroads; those in power are determined to invade the church and force Christ's followers to do what their consciences will not allow. But Chuck — the man who voluntarily confessed to a Watergate-related crime knowing he would likely be sent to prison as a result — insisted that we love God no matter what the cost.*

*As his dear friend Father Richard Neuhaus, who died three years before Chuck, had put it: "Undaunted, we are enlisted for the duration and bearing witness to the truth."*

I personally am very glad to be here because this is the first time I've been out in three months. I had a little mishap and have been on the sidelines recuperating. So I'm really glad. I would not have wanted to miss this weekend, and was afraid I might have to.

I happen to be one of those who believe that societies are changed by movements at the grassroots. So how do we get that material out to people so they can use it for their neighbors? I think cultures are changed over the backyard fence and the barbecue grill; I don't believe they're changed from the top down. And I'll talk to you tonight a little bit about why I think that is so critical right now.

My topic is the cultural environment today. Culture at a crossroads, which indeed it is. What you've just witnessed with the Department of Health and Human Services attempting to impose a mandate on the church and Christian groups and religious organizations, forcing them to provide insurance for things that violate our conscience, and not allowing a conscience exemption. What's extraordinary about that is there have been battles over religious liberty ever since the nation was founded. Most of them have ended up in court decisions, sometimes legislative. This is the first time in history—which is why Cardinal Donald Wuerl here in Washington said this is the most serious invasion of the church by government, ever—it's the first time it's been done by a bureaucrat in a government agency simply writing it and putting it out as law. Normally in a court case you get a chance to argue both sides. But there wasn't a chance for two sides to be argued this time; it was done by executive fiat.

But it's opportune for us as we meet here tonight. Eric Metaxas said this is a moment. This is a moment where the church has to learn how to defend itself against this sort of thing, and do it in a sort of way that is constructive.

What we're witnessing in our culture today—the HHS mandate is but the tip of the iceberg. It's the latest visible manifestation of a growing hostility to Christianity. Mainly because—and this has always been the case—government officials feel threatened by the power of the church, because we all worship a King higher than the kings of this earth. And that's seen as a threat.

We're also seen as wanting to impose our views on people. Don't let them tell you that. We don't impose anything; we propose. We propose an invitation to the wedding feast, to come to a better way of living. A better way of life. It's the great proposal. We couldn't impose if we wanted to impose. And we don't want to impose. In our democracy, you can't.

So we need to be very clear about who we are and what we do and why we do it. I hope some of the teaching this weekend will help you with that. But what we're seeing now is the fruits that have come from thirty years of relativism, the death of truth, in the academy particularly, and in public discourse. And the coarsening of public discourse, the coarsening of politics.

Everybody looks to the elections and thinks, well, the elections are going to settle this problem or settle that problem. Elections are important. Whoever serves in office, it makes a difference what kind of person that is and what that person believes. But elections can't solve the problems we've got. The problem we've got is that our culture has been decaying from the inside out for thirty or forty years....

# EPILOGUE

*Chuck's death was a shock to those of us who had worked for him for many years. He swam daily in Naples, Florida, and kept to a healthy diet. We joked that this man, a generation older than we were, had more energy than the rest of us put together.*

*Chuck's life was a living testament to the power of Christ to change lives: the Watergate felon who created a dark and destructive atmosphere in the Nixon White House was transformed into the man who voluntarily went into thousands of the world's prisons to pray with inmates and bring them into the kingdom of God.*

# NOTES

## Apologetics

1. *Orthodoxy* was originally published in 1908 and is available online and in numerous print editions. This quotation is from chapter 6, "The Paradoxes of Christianity."

2. Ibid.

3. Ibid.

## Bioethics and Life Issues

1. http://en.wikipedia.org/wiki/Euthanasia_in_the_Netherlands.

2. *Compassion in Dying v. State of Washington*, No. 94–35534 (9th Cir. 1996).

3. Ariel Kaminer, "Abortion: Easy Access, Complex Everything Else," *New York Times*, January 21, 2011, http://www.nytimes.com/2011/01/23/nyregion/23critic.html?_r=0.

4. Eric Metaxas, *Bonhoeffer* (Nashville: Thomas Nelson, 2011), 184.

5. Ibid.

## Christians and Public Life

1. Adam Cohen, "Four Decades After Milgram, We're Still Willing to Inflict Pain," *New York Times*, December 28, 2008, http://www.nytimes.com/2008/12/29/opinion/29mon3.html.

2. Martin Luther King Jr., "Letter from a Birmingham Jail," April 16, 1963. In his letter to clergymen, Dr. King explains that there are two types of laws: just and unjust. He continues, "I would agree with St. Augustine that 'an unjust law is no law at all.'"

3. "Let every person be subject to the governing authorities. For there is no authority except from God, and those that exist have been instituted by God.... For rulers are not a terror to good conduct, but to bad" (Romans 13:1, 3 ESV).

4. Harvey Mansfield, "Atheist Tracts," *The Weekly Standard* 12, no. 45 (August 13, 2007), http://www.weeklystandard.com/Content/Public/Articles/000/000/013/954gkvmp.asp?page=1.

## Church and Culture

1. Andrew Osborn, "As If Things Weren't Bad Enough, Russian Professor Predicts End of U.S.," *Wall Street Journal*, December 29, 2008, http://online.wsj.com/news/articles/SB123051100709638419.

2. Meghan Cox Gurdon, "Emily Post Would Be Rightly Appalled," *Wall Street Journal*, February 5, 2010, http://online.wsj.com/news/articles/SB2000142405274870432010457501513343210118.

3. David McCasland, *Oswald Chambers: Abandon to God: The Life Story of the Author of* My Utmost for His Highest (Charlotte: Billy Graham Evangelistic Association, 1979).

4. "Doing the Right Thing" can be ordered from www.Colson Centerstore.org.

5. Michael B. Barkey, ed., *Environmental Stewardship in the Judeo-Christian Tradition* (Grand Rapids: Acton Institute, 2008).

6. Chuck visited Northern Ireland in 1977. In his book *Kingdoms in Conflict*, Chuck discusses this turbulent time.

## Crime, Punishment, and Justice

1. "For when we were in the realm of the flesh, the sinful passions aroused by the law were at work in us, so that we bore fruit for death" (Romans 7:5).

2. James Q. Wilson and Richard J. Hernstein, *Crime and Human Nature* (New York: Simon & Schuster, 1985).

3. Ibid

4. See Wade F. Horn and David Blankenhorn, *The Fatherhood Movement: A Call to Action* (Lanham, MD: Rowman & Littlesield, 199).

5. "I do not understand what I do. For what I want to do I do not do, but what I hate I do" (Romans 7:15).

## Happiness

1. Bret Stephens, "Richest Country, Saddest People. Any Coincidence?" *Wall Street Journal*, March 9, 2007, http://www.wsj.com/articles/SB117341542798232054.

2. D. T. Max, "Happiness 101," *New York Times*, January 7, 2007, http://www.nytimes.com/2007/01/07/magazine/07happiness.t.html?pagewanted=all.

3. Robert Bellah, *Habits of the Heart* (Los Angeles: University of California Press, 1996).

## Homosexuality and the Church

1. Robert P. George, "Ashamed of the Gospel?" National Catho-

lic Prayer Breakfast, May 13, 2014, http://www.catholicprayerbreak
fast.com/2014/robert_george_remarks_2014.pdf.

2. Robert P. George, "The Clash of Orthodoxy," *First Things*, August 1999, http://www.firstthings.com/article/1999/08/a-clash -of-orthodoxies. See also, Sherif Girgis, Ryan T. Anderson, Robert P. George, *What Is Marriage?* (Encounter Books: New York, 2012).

3. Jennifer Roback Morse, "The Institution Formerly Known as Marriage," PublicDiscourse.com, April 24, 2009, http://www.thepub licdiscourse.com/2009/04/234/. See also Jennifer Roback Morse, "Prepared remarks for the Illinois state legislature, hearings on SB 10," February 26, 2013, http://www.ruthblog.org/2013/02/27/prepared -remarks-for-the-illinois-state-legislature-hearings-on-sb–10/.

4. J. Budziszewski, "So-Called Gay Marriage: A Dialogue," Boundless.org, February 19, 2004, http://www.boundless.org/ relationships/2004/so-called-marriage. See also J. Budziszewski, *On the Meaning of Sex* (Wilmington, Del.: Intercollegiate Studies Institute, 2012).

5. Phillip E. Johnson is Professor of Law, Emeritus, at the University of California, Berkeley School of Law, and is the father of the Intelligent Design movement.

6. This is especially timely given Obama's executive order this week. Peter Baker, "President Calls for a Ban on Job Bias Against Gays," *New York Times*, July 21, 2014, http://www.nytimes .com/2014/07/22/us/politics/obama-job-discrimination-gays -executive-order.html?_r=0.

7. Chuck Colson, "So Now It's Freedom of Religion?" Break-Point Radio, September 1, 2010, http://www.breakpoint.org/ bpcommentaries/breakpoint-commentaries-search/entry/13/15213.

8. Joe McGinness, "Eagelton Seemed Superficial," *Daytona Beach Morning Journal*, May 7, 1973, http://news.google.com/ newspapers?nid=1873&dat=19730507&id=AE4fAAAAIBAJ&sjid=m9E EAAAAIBAJ&pg=4270,2887692.

9. Stanley Kurtz, "The End of Marriage in Scandinavia," *Weekly Standard*, February 2, 2004, http://www.weeklystandard.com/ Content/Public/Articles/000/000/003/660zypwj.asp.

10. Laurie Goodstein, "At Axis of the Episcopal Split, an Anti-gay Nigerian," *New York Times*, December 25, 2006, http:// www.nytimes.com/2006/12/25/world/africa/25episcopal.html? pagewanted=all&_r=0.

11. Steve Rempe, "A Historic Gathering of Anglicans," Break-Point.org, June 22, 2009, http://www.breakpoint.org/component/ blog/entry/4/1816.

12. The Book of Nature, a Middle Ages religious concept, suggests we view nature as a "book" that can be "read" for an understanding of the world.

## Islam versus Christianity

1. Samuel P. Huntington, "The Clash of Civilizations?" *Foreign Affairs*, Summer 1993, http://www.svt.ntnu.no/iss/Indra.de.Soysa/POL2003H05/huntington_clash%20of%20civlizations.pdf . He fleshed out his thesis into a book: *The Clash of Civilizations and the Remaking of World Order* (New York: Random House, 2007).

2. According to an ICM poll, 20 percent of British Muslims sympathize with those who committed the July 7 attacks; one in four believes the attacks were justified, http://freethoughtblogs.com/taslima/2013/08/03/unfortunately-a-large-number-of-muslims-support-terrorism911womens-oppressionsharia-lawshonor-killings/.

3. Thomas L. Friedman, "Martin Luther Al-King?" *New York Times*, January 24, 2007, http://www.nytimes.com/2007/01/24/opinion/24friedman.html.

4. Richard Bonney, *False Prophets: The "Clash of Civilizations" and the Global War on Terror* (Oxford, England: Peter Lang, 2008), 43.

5. Deuteronomy 7:1–2; 20:16–18.

6. Daniel Pipes, "British Culture—Worth Saving?" July 14, 2005, http://www.danielpipes.org/blog/2005/07/british-culture-worth-saving. See also Anthony Brown, "The Left's War on Britishness," July 23, 2005, http://www.spectator.co.uk/features/13940/the-lefts-war-on-britishness/ , and Aatish Taseer, "A British Jihadist," *Prospect*, August 28, 2005, http://www.prospectmagazine.co.uk/features/a-british-jihadist-hassan-butt.

7. David Aikman, *Jesus in Beijing* (Washington, DC: Regnery, 2006).

8. Jon Meacham, "The Pope's 'Holy War,'" *Newsweek*, September 25, 2006, http://www.newsweek.com/popes-holy-war-109455.

9. "An Open Letter and Call from Muslim Religious Leaders," October 13, 2007, http://www.acommonword.com/the-letter-of-138-muslim-scholars-to-the-pope-and-christian-leaders/.

10. Pope Benedict XVI, "Faith, Reason, and the University," September 12, 2006, http://www.vatican.va/holy_father/benedict_xvi/speeches/2006/september/documents/hf_ben-xvi_spe_20060912_university-regensburg_en.html.

11. "Loving God and Neighbor Together: A Christian Response to a Common Word Between Us and You," *New York Times*, October 13, 2007, See number 32, http://www.acommonword.com/category/site/christian-responses/.

## Judicial Usurpation

1. John Leo, "An Elite Legal Culture Runs Over Democracy," *Herald-Journal*, May 13, 1997.

2. Linda Greenhouse, "A Turf Battle's Unlikely Victim," *New York Times*, June 28, 2000, http://www.nytimes.com/2000/06/28/us/a -turf-battle-s-unlikely-victim.html.

3. The Religious Liberty Protection Act was passed in 1999. See Chuck Colson, "A Debt of Gratitude," BreakPoint Radio, July 21, 1999, https://www.breakpoint.org/commentaries/5336-a-debt-of-gratitude.

4. Chuck was speaking about Congressman Charles Canady (R-FL) and Congressman Henry Hyde (R-IL).

5. Congressman John Lewis (D-GA).

## Blessed are the Poor

1. Leon Kass, *The Beginning of Wisdom: Reading Genesis* (New York: Free Press, 2003), 242.

2. Henry Fairlie, *The Seven Deadly Sins Today* (Notre Dame: University of Notre Dame Press, 1979), 61.

## Persecution

1. In 1997, Jiang Zemin was the president of China. On *BreakPoint Radio,* Chuck spoke out about Zemin's visit to the US. Chuck Colson, "China to U.S.: Shut-up on Human Rights," BreakPoint Radio, October 30, 1997, http://www.breakpoint.org/ commentaries/4730-china-to-us.

2. Steve Gushee, "Using the Bible to Support the Wrong Cause," *Palm Beach Post*, December 2004.

3. Charles Austin, "Colson's Call to Convert Muslims Is Dangerous," *Bergen Record*, February 14, 2002.

4. Steven Lee Myers, "More Christians Are Fleeing Iraq After New Violence," *New York Times*, December 12, 2010, http:// www.nytimes.com/2010/12/13/world/middleeast/13iraq. html?pagewanted=all&_r=0.

## Suffering

1. L. B. Cowman, *Streams in the Desert*, ed. Jim Reimann (Grand Rapids: Zondervan, 2008), 245.

2. Ibid., 415.

3. Ibid., 416.

4. Agnieszka Tennant, "Brave New Salvation," *Christianity Today*, June 20, 2007, http://www.christianitytoday.com/ct/2007/ june/22.64.html.

5. Amy Harmon, "Six Billion Bits of Data About Me, Me, Me,"

*New York Times,* June 3, 2007, http://www.nytimes.com/2007/06/03/weekinreview/03harm.html?_r=0.

## War of the Worldviews

1. Lionel Tiger, "Is the Supernatural Only Natural?" *Wall Street Journal,* March 27, 2010.

2. Ibid

3. Chuck Colson, "Answering Four Questions," Two-Minute Warning, April 6, 2011, http://www.colsoncenter.org/twominutewarning/archive/entry/33/16804. You can also access a copy of the grid by going to the Colson Center Library, http://www.colsoncenter.org/search-library/search?view=searchdetail&id=18534.

4. Richard Dawkins, *The God Delusion* (Boston: Houghton Mifflin, 2006); William Dennett, *Breaking the Spell* (New York: Viking, 2006); Christopher Hitchens, *God Is Not Great* (New York: Grand Central, 2009).

5. Robert Barro, "Bill Gates's Charitable Vistas," *Wall Street Journal,* June 19, 2007, http://online.wsj.com/news/articles/SB118222027751440041.

6. Matt Ridley, "Humans: Why They Triumphed," *Wall Street Journal,* May 22, 2010, http://online.wsj.com/news/articles/SB10001424052748703691804575254533386933138.

7. Rodney Stark, *The Victory of Reason: How Christianity Led to Freedom, Capitalism, and Western Success* (New York: Random House, 2005).

8. Arthur Brooks, "Our Religious Destiny," American Enterprise Institute, http://www.aei.org/publication/our-religious-destiny-2/.

9. Rodney Stark, *The Rise of Christianity: How the Obscure, Marginal Jesus Movement Became the Dominant Religious Force in the Western World in a Few Centuries* (San Francisco: HarperSanFrancisco, 1997).

# The Faith

## What Christians Believe, Why They Believe It, and Why It Matters

*Charles Colson and Harold Fickett*

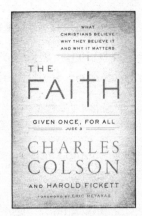

Rightly understood and rightly communicated, the Christian faith is one of great joy. It is an invitation to God's kingdom, where tears are replaced by laughter and longing hearts find their purpose and their home. This is the heart of the gospel: God's search to reclaim us and love us as his own. But have we truly grasped this? Those of us who have disdained Christianity as a religion of bigotry—have we repudiated the genuine article or merely demonstrated our own prejudice and ignorance? Those of us who are Christians—have we deeply apprehended the mission of Jesus, and do our ways and character faithfully reflect his beauty?

From the nature of God, to the human condition, to the work of Jesus, to God's coming kingdom, and all that lies between, how well do we understand the foundational truths of Christianity and their implications? *The Faith* is a book for our troubled times and for decades to come, for Christians and non-Christians alike. It is the most important book Chuck Colson and Harold Fickett have ever written: a thought-provoking, soul-searching, and powerful manifesto of the great, historical central truths of Christianity that have sustained believers through the centuries. Brought to immediacy with vivid, true stories, here is what Christianity is really about and why it is a religion of hope, redemption, and beauty.

*Available in stores and online!*

# God and Government

## An Insider's View on the Boundaries between Faith and Politics

*Charles Colson*

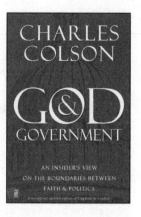

How should Christians live their faith in the public arena?

Twenty years ago, the first edition of Chuck Colson's *Kingdoms in Conflict* became a bestseller, a must-read for people interested in politics and the relationship between church and state. Now, with a passion for truth and moved by the urgency of the times we live in, Colson has written *God and Government*, re-voicing his powerful and enduring message for our post-9/11 world.

In an era when Christianity is being attacked from every side—books being written charging Christians with being theocrats and trying to impose their views on an unwilling culture—what is the message of the Christian church? What does the Bible say, and what do we learn from history about the proper relationship between faith and culture? Appealing to Scripture, reason, and history, this book tackles society's most pressing and divisive issues. New stories and examples reflect the realities of today, from the clash with radical Islam to the deep division between "reds" and "blues." In an era of angry finger-pointing, Colson furnishes a unique insider's perspective that can't be pigeonholed as either "religious right" or "religious left."

Whatever your political or religious stance, this book will give you a different understanding of Christianity. If you're a Christian, it will help you to both examine and defend your faith. If you've been critical of the new religious right, you'll be shocked at what you learn. Probing both secular and religious values, *God and Government* critiques each fairly, sides with neither, and offers a hopeful, fair-minded perspective that is sorely needed in today's hyper-charged atmosphere.

*Available in stores and online!*

**ZONDERVAN®**
.com

# Loving God

*Charles Colson*

In his magnificent classic, Chuck Colson shakes
the church from its complacency with a penetrat-
ing look at the cost of being Christian. For those
who have wondered whether there isn't more to
Christianity than what they have known—and for
those who have never considered the question—
*Loving God* points the way to faith's cutting edge.
Here is a compelling, probing look at the cost of discipleship and the
meaning of the first and greatest commandment—one that will strum a
deeper, truer chord within even as it strips away the trappings of shallow,
cultural Christianity.

> *"Looking for the complete volume on Christian living? This is it. And the
> title sums it up. If you desire life deep, rich, and meaningful, then it is
> simply* Loving God.*"*
>
> —Joni Eareckson Tada President, Joni and Friends